Yael Ben-Da~~v~~

THE BUSINESS
OF UX WRITING

All rights reserved
Publisher: Jeffrey Zeldman
Designer: Jason Santa Maria
Executive director: Katel LeDû
Managing editor: Lisa Maria Marquis
Editors: Sharina Wunderink, Susan Bond, Kumari Pacheco, Caren Litherland
Book producer: Ron Bilodeau

ISBN: 978-1-952616-24-2

A Book Apart
New York, New York
http://abookapart.com

10 9 8 7 6 5 4 3 2 1

TABLE OF CONTENTS

Introduction

CHAPTER 1
4 A Short Biography of UX Writing

CHAPTER 2
25 Where UX Writing and Business Meet

CHAPTER 3
46 How UX Writing Increases ROI

CHAPTER 4
70 Show Me the Money: Measuring Success

CHAPTER 5
96 Impacting the Business Beyond UX Writing

But Wait, There's More!

Acknowledgments

Resources

References

Index

For Maya, Adelle, and Ori

I'M ONE OF THOSE UX writers who has gone too far. I've advocated for the user experience to have more investment, more care, more consideration for the user—and I've done it loudly, angrily, toe-to-toe with the business decision-maker.

But there is a smarter way, and it's *together*. I didn't understand it then, but the business decision-makers—the PMs, general managers, and C-suite stakeholders of my teams—usually know that they need the user as much as I do. And to get the user, they need my content team's skill set. If we don't engage the user, the business needs won't be met at the rate the company hopes for.

In this book, Yael Ben-David neatly articulates the struggle so many of us UX writers face in "getting a seat at the table"— then challenges us to focus on using that seat. Yael provides practical frameworks to equip UX writers to deliver a solid return on the business' UX writing investment. These frameworks encourage us to think beyond the user, to the broader context of the business and its ethical ramifications—all while modeling how to use the common language of business to drive alignment with our cross-functional stakeholders.

I predict that this book, and the ideas in it, will nudge UX writing (and content design) into more effective, more valuable work. I'm looking forward to the impact this book will have on our discipline. We will have a groundswell of people measuring, experimenting, publishing, and sharing their best UX writing thinking.

If you want to use UX writing to do more for your customer, your business, and your peers—you're in the right place. Turn the page.

—Torrey Podmajersky

OVER THE PAST FEW DECADES, digital products have advanced immensely on all fronts. The technology is better, the user experience is better, the chances of going viral are higher. However, having each front improve in a silo is not going to be enough for the next great leap forward. It's time to harness the power of interdisciplinary collaboration and lateral thinking, to take a holistic approach to our day-to-day work. We need to move past the mindset that assumes we succeed by winning resources from other contributors and earning priority at their expense. Everyone working on a digital product shares the same ultimate goal, so why not focus on how our area of expertise can benefit our partners' work—and reach new heights together?

As we make that paradigm shift and put collaboration at the core of our approach, we also must prioritize the interests of our users or our business. In my area of expertise, user experience writing (UXW), there has been a historical tension between serving the user and serving the business. This book aims to turn that around. UX writers, users, and businesses are interconnected. Users need businesses to build products they can use, while businesses need users' engagement to succeed. When we craft product copy solutions, we shouldn't be split between a version that best serves the user and one that best serves the business; our solution should serve the goals of both, which are shared.

A poignant example of how user needs serve business interests—as opposed to competing with them for resources—comes from Doug Dietz's journey in designing MRI equipment for hospitals. When he first began, he designed machines to the highest medical and technological standards. This made the business and product teams happy, but some child patients would not get into the machine. Before Dietz came along, 80 percent of child patients were being sedated to get through their MRI. Wait lists were long because nervous children needed to be coaxed through the procedure, a slow and emotionally painful task. Although these user pain points directly affected business metrics (in that more MRIs carried out at a faster rate would lead to more profit), earlier designs had not prioritized them. Dietz was faced with a question: Would investing in users' comfort take away from product and business needs? After all, there's a cost to investing in users' comfort.

He went back to the drawing board, returning with a wildly reconsidered set of MRIs. Each machine was painted to resemble a different setting: river, jungle, ship, campsite. Sounds, smells, and images enriched the experience and encouraged helpful behaviors. For example, children were incentivized to stay still—critical to the success of the scan—not by their parents begging them to be brave, but by the promise of magical fish that would "jump" over them if they didn't rock the "canoe." Whatever it cost the business to invest—in elaborate paintings, aromas, and more—it was worth it.

Suddenly, fewer than 1 percent of children needed to be sedated. Patient satisfaction went up by 92 percent. Tests ran faster, which meant wait lists were shorter. The machines grew popular with hospitals and patients alike, leading to a success that would have been impossible had Dietz seen each side's needs as being in conflict, where each could only succeed at the expense of the other. He had found a way to satisfy both, and more, by focusing on joint incentives. I highly recommend watching his full TED Talk (https://bkaprt.com/buxw43/00-01, video).

In UXW, we often tussle with this perceived conflict between serving the user and serving the business. For example, we may argue that personalization in user-facing communications is best for users, while, to the business, investing engineering resources to that end is wasteful. Advocating for the user can feel like an uphill battle, and it's easy to resent the stakeholders we perceive to be minimizing the value of investing in these needs. But it's time to change our mindset. All of us.

In my work as a UX writer, I've been privileged with opportunities that explore the often overlooked dynamic between UXW and business interests. I am frequently the only speaker at conferences addressing UXW from a business perspective as opposed to the end users', and, as far as I know, there is no book out there yet dedicated to this topic. As the field grows, we can and should dive deeper into different areas—and I've been exploring this one.

Whatever shape UXW takes in your life, this book brings a fresh perspective that can improve your process and grow your impact.

Good luck!

1

A SHORT BIOGRAPHY OF UX WRITING

UXW ROLES HAVE BEEN growing in number and responsibilities around the world, every year, for over a decade. When I was looking for a UXW job in 2018 in Tel Aviv, a global high-tech hub, I received on average one LinkedIn alert a day. A few short years later, I get dozens. The demand for UXW is growing for one simple reason: good UXW is good for business.

Before I go on about how wonderful UXW is, and what a relief it is that the world is finally starting to value it, let's define it to make sure we're all on the same page:

UXW is the creation and maintenance of product content.

UXW is as core to user experience as visual design, and likewise requires intimate collaboration with UX researchers and product managers to provide a product experience that meets, and ideally exceeds, users' needs and goals.

Specifically, UX writers (also called content designers) are responsible for writing and helping structure the presentation of *microcopy*: all of the bits of text that appear in the product itself—on buttons, in menus, on form-field labels and place-holders, for product experiences that happen on screens, and in scripts for chatbots and voice interfaces (also known as conversation design). UX writers also create copy to support the user journey outside of the product interface—items like transactional emails, SMS text, and push notifications.

When UX writers aren't writing, they're measuring and optimizing what they've written, building and maintaining systems of process, collaboration, and documentation toward durable scalability (content operations). UX writers also manage the product's voice and tone.

That's a lot. It's stuff that has been necessary ever since digital experiences first emerged, but there was not always someone doing it. Back in the day, user experience didn't matter too much, because there was a power imbalance in which people needed digital products more than the products needed them, and there were so few users anyway that requiring users to accommodate digital products—instead of designing products to accommodate users—worked okay.

That has all changed.

THE BEGINNING

Let's start with when computers entered the consumer space in earnest.

The PC revolution

In the 1980s, the personal computing revolution put pressure on the computer industry to improve the usability of its products (https://bkaprt.com/buxw43/01-01). All of a sudden there were way more users, and they were using digital products to spend money directly. For digital products to succeed, users could no longer be expected to overcome the learning curve of working with this technology; the products had to conform to the way users worked. Finally, humans could stop speaking computer because computers were starting to speak human.

This also raised the stakes for user experience; better usability translated directly into sales, and the companies behind these digital products needed sales to survive. User needs and business needs became coupled. Either they both won or they both lost.

As the PC revolution ran its course, it became commonplace for people to own personal computers. In contrast to most product experiences today, digital products of this era were sold first and experienced later. In other words, you'd be convinced to purchase software without trying it out first, likely receiving it as a disc that you'd then put in your computer's CD drive and install. By the time you started to experience the product, the business already had your money. That was before the web.

The web revolution

In the 1990s, the web revolution made good UX even more critical. Instead of purchasing software first and experiencing its interface later, users would interact with a website before deciding whether or not to buy the software (https://bkaprt. com/buxw43/01-01). Now businesses had to create a digital product experience that ended in a completed purchase, not the other way around.

Don Norman, considered one of the founding fathers of UX, coined the term *user experience* (UX) in 1993. You could say that this is when the UX discipline first gained traction; suddenly businesses had to start caring about users' interactions with their digital products and define them more tangibly (https://bkaprt.com/buxw43/01-01). Since then, the field of UX has grown and matured, and subspecialties have arisen, primarily *UX design* (UXD), *UX research* (UXR), and *UX writing* (UXW).

UX writing becomes a thing

The practice of UX writing started decades before it had a name. For as long as there have been words on screens, people have been writing for users. Product creators started to care more about those words in the 1990s, putting significant thought into writing them. That doesn't mean they went so far as to hire an expert. There weren't any experts yet. No one had been thinking about it long enough, so non-UX writers were doing UXW. Unfortunately, even today, not all companies have a dedicated role for UXW. In the absence of UX writers, this work is being done by technical writers, content writers specializing in longer out-of-product pieces like blog posts, and even visual designers, product managers, and (in desperate moments) engineers.

UX writing becomes an actual thing

As UX increasingly came into focus and UXW gained recognition as a specialty within it, the practice was officially named. Best practices, like clarity and concision (https://bkaprt.com/buxw43/01-02, video), were developed and codified, and the first books dedicated to UXW came out. UXW was represented at UX conferences, and, later, dedicated UXW conferences were established. Courses and bootcamps started popping up as a way for people to get started in the field, because there was no designated path to this new career. It became clear that the field was maturing—becoming more robust, purposeful, and impactful.

Today, almost all leading high-tech companies have at least one dedicated UX writer and are adding to that number every year—some companies like Meta and Wix have hundreds. UXW courses are being added to college curricula. Discussions about upward mobility, management roles, and longer-term career paths are among the newest topics appearing in UXW forums all over.

UX writing goes too far

As UXW became a mainstream, dedicated role with a recognized, specialized skill set, UX writers from across dozens of job titles finally had a common identity, which was quickly followed by community. The spirit of our new role was to *put the user first*, always. We invested in research to understand what makes product copy easiest for users to consume, digest, and understand. What makes users comfortable? What delights them? What improves their experience for the sake of improving their experience and puts them at the center for once? We finally started listening to users and integrating their language into our user interfaces, sometimes verbatim. It wasn't 1980 anymore; it was time to put the user in the spotlight!

Given this context, UXW was largely reactionary, a revolution against the days of typing `c : / /` in DOS. But we forgot an important aspect of this user-centered revolution: the benefit to the business. Once customers used products first and purchased them later, businesses had to improve their UX to make sales. It was not a move made from the goodness of the businesses' hearts; they did it because there is a direct connection between better user experience and more successful business. Somehow, though, between 1980 and 2020, that part of the picture got lost. It's easy to think we're waging a chronic war on behalf of users and at the expense of the business, but nothing could be further from the truth. As a business succeeds and grows, its ability to serve users' needs also grows. How is this not in the users' best interest? We've gone too far, becoming myopic in our advocacy for the user.

To demonstrate this point on a very small scale, consider a team deciding whether to personalize emails. "Hi Mo," instead of "Hi," seems like a better UX decision. However, coding that string means querying the backend to pull the variable "Mo" from a database. Now, fallbacks are needed for when that information is missing, and CSS rules need to be set for when the user-generated input includes errors, like names written in all caps or starting with a lowercase letter. Say all of this amounts to $50,000 in development costs. Is it still a good idea? UX zealots might say yes: that we should always optimize the experience, at all costs. But as a user, I'd rather the business invest $50,000 in a new feature than in showing me my name.

There is always a trade-off; nothing is free. For every dollar and hour we're investing in one area, we're not investing in another. UXW is no different; it too has a *return on investment* (ROI) that needs to be measured for the benefit of the user and business alike. Once we consider how "user-centered" improvements to UXW often cost resources that could've been invested elsewhere—and with a higher return for both the user and the business—the conversation surrounding UX copy becomes more nuanced.

It's time to correct the well-meaning practice of overshooting in the direction of user-centered copy; the pendulum has swung too far. We need to strike a balance that solves user needs in a more comprehensive way, by leveraging the most powerful contributor to their success: the business.

UX WRITERS TODAY

As UX writers today, we need to harness our collective strength and passion to make this shift, and we're already making great strides.

Documenting what we know

On a *Designed Today* podcast episode, guest Torrey Podmajersky described the moment she decided to write her book, *Strategic Writing for UX* (2019). She was sitting at a table with UX writers over lunch at Confab, a content strategy conference, and heard people discussing problems that her team had already solved (https://bkaprt.com/buxw43/01-03). She realized a few things, namely that UX writers need:

- A way to stop reinventing the wheel and instead funnel our collective energy into moving our discipline forward
- A way to share successes and brainstorm together about how to overcome shared challenges

So she wrote a book, considered a must-read in our industry, chronicling lessons learned for others to build on. Documentation, in the form of blogs, books, and talks, has continued to grow since then.

Developing evidence-based best practices

The same year Podmajersky documented a strategic framework for us all to use as a baseline, Kinneret Yifrah published *Microcopy: The Complete Guide*, finally collecting and publishing tactical best practices. The book doubles as a common starting point for new UX writers and a set of heuristics for current UX writers to align themselves with. As of the writing of this book, *Microcopy* has been translated into six languages and shipped to more than fifty countries. People are excited to start, and they're desperate to know how. Between Podmajersky setting us up to align on strategy and Yifrah giving us a handbook on tactics, we are well on our way.

That said, plenty of conventions have been updated over time, based on data. To do our job well, we need to keep up with the research—and contribute our own findings, too. It's up to each of us to take ownership of UXW and the learnings generated from it, growing the pool of communal knowledge.

However, this is easier said than done when we owe our allegiance to a particular employer, or when we're busy as free-lancers making sure we're bringing in the business we need for ourselves first. Until we get an organization like the National Institutes of Health (NIH) that hands out grants for conducting medical research for the greater good, we need to make time for research and knowledge sharing during our day jobs. We'll need to justify our research as pertinent to our specific employer, but then share how it applies more generally.

Take, for example, the conversation around capitalization best practices: When should we use sentence case? (Almost always.) Is there ever an excuse to use all caps? (Very rarely.) When should we use title case? (Depends on whom you ask.) Consensus needs to be based on evidence. To that end, Microsoft has conducted some of the most rigorous research on casing, using tools like fast eye trackers, to present the science that validates or invalidates common UXW heuristics (https://bkaprt.com/buxw43/01-04). They found that text in all caps doesn't always affect readability like we thought, and that when it does, it may have more to do with what we're used to than some physiological limitation concerning letter and word shapes.

The same Microsoft research addressed qualitative metrics for vague buzzwords like "scannability" that we all throw around. For example, they found that our eyes skip over short words all together (**FIG 1.1**). We may not need to be so concerned

Roadside joggers endure sweat, pain and angry drivers in

the name of fitness. A healthy body may seem reward...

FIG 1.1: Microsoft published a diagram of the fixation points of a typical reader (saccadic eye movements) showing that our eyes tend to skip over short words, take in medium-sized words as a whole and not letter by letter, and periodically go backward and revisit words we've already read.

about an extra short word in a call to action (CTA); turns out, it's not actually holding up the user at all.

Similarly, Google shared data about a test they did on their hotel search widget copy (**FIG 1.2**). They hypothesized that the copy "Book a room" was too committal and did not empathize with users' mindset at that point in the flow. Users were not ready to book a room; they simply wanted to browse. Google backed up their hypothesis with data: a 17 percent increase in conversion when they lowered the perceived commitment of the touchpoint from "Book a room" to "Check availability." Note that the functionality did not change, only the microcopy. Maybe they were hypothesizing about copy tweaks that would increase a very specific Google metric, but along the way, they provided us all with data that showed the value of copy that not only tells users what to do and how to do it, but also resonates with what they're thinking at the time (https://bkaprt.com/buxw43/01-05, video).

Data-backed tests like these do wonders for convincing stakeholders to invest in copy changes. I later used this research to support making microcopy changes in my own work. There was a CTA—"Draw Funds"—that users had to click or tap on in order to continue along a Draw Funds flow (**FIG 1.3**). When I read the Google research, I realized that our users might also be hesitant to engage because "Draw Funds" felt too committal. The next screen did not actually transfer funds to the user's

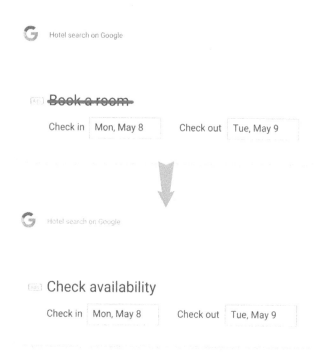

FIG 1.2: Google shares impressive qualitative results from their UXW test.

bank account; it showed them the details of their options for repaying the funds they were about to borrow. Only *after* reviewing and confirming would they get to the CTA that initiated the transfer. We changed the button from "Draw Funds" to "Review and Draw."

We were able to implement this improvement because we had data, like the Google stat, to support the decision. This is exactly why it's so important for us to do and share research within the UXW community. We got feedback that the change was helpful from our user-facing teams, who had first raised the flag after conversations with users who wanted to draw funds but were scared of the "Draw Funds" CTA—users who converted immediately did so after the reps explained to them that in fact, only "Review" would come next. Users benefited

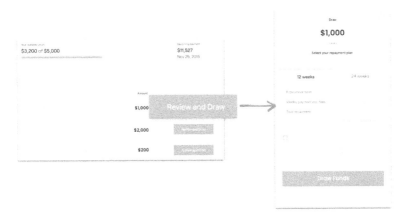

FIG 1.3: Based on Google's test results, we made some microcopy changes and saw similar success.

from this change because they were now able to complete the flow with peace of mind. And of course, users drawing funds is in the business's best interest as well.

Google's research about empathetic copy was not the only research we applied to this work. In our first iteration, we used an ampersand: "Review & Draw." We then applied research from Content London's global, community-sourced, evidence-based wiki, the Readability Guidelines, which suggests that ampersands are not accessible or inclusive, and that wherever possible, spelling out "and" is strongly recommended. Our next iteration, "Review and Draw," reflected this.

While applying Microsoft, Google, and Readability Guidelines research to my work, I also aimed to put my own research out into the world for others. I looked at the effect of microcopy on perceived trustworthiness. The project focused on a specific touchpoint in a particular flow where we hypothesized that drop-off could be decreased if we better addressed users' concerns about trust. It makes sense that research by any in-house UX writer will be supported only if there are direct, relevant, and impactful implications for their organization's product. However, UX writers everywhere can benefit from data on how

Control variant

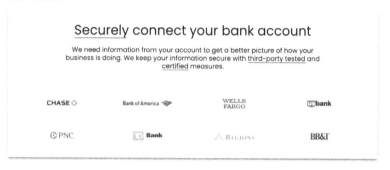

Test variant

FIG 1.4: Based on research, we ran a microcopy test around users' concerns about our product's security, better communicating mechanisms that were already in place.

their words affect users' likelihood to trust, and in turn, engage long-term with their products.

For example, I found that using simple "trust buzzwords" makes a difference (Fig 1.4). I rewrote copy without changing the messaging or functionality—simply adding words like "securely" and "certified"—and asked test participants how likely they were to trust our product after reading each version. It's important to reiterate that the "before" and "after" copy examples were equally true, equally reflective of the existing security mechanisms like active security certifications, and both in place specifically to address users' expressed concerns. But the exact language was not the same, and that made a difference.

It wasn't up to me to put the security mechanisms in place, but it *was* up to me to talk about them in a way that resonated with, informed, and served users. After all, users were on this screen to apply for credit, and they wanted to get it done. We needed them to complete this flow as part of our onboarding. Microcopy that helped reduce friction on this screen was good for everyone, and buzzwords played a big role in that.

The effect of buzzwords may not seem rational, but the data speaks for itself. Like any other tool, they're helpful when used at the right moment. Think about it: our employers are already investing in us to write; writing with trust buzzwords costs nothing extra but can increase the return. I was inspired to test this hypothesis after reading about how a car company increased conversions by simply adding a frame to the end of a TV commercial that said, "Trust us." That's it. Just the word "trust" made a difference.

With data to back us up, we can push changes like these, even if there's initial pushback about the approach not being worth the design real estate or the engineering cost. That's why it's important we all contribute research, especially if it's research our organizations will sponsor (because they'll benefit from it) and that our industry lacks. For example, I justified my project with the promise that the findings would have an immediate impact on an important touchpoint in my product's flow. Of course, this research also benefited the greater UXW community, better equipping us to improve the ROI for our own businesses. Building a robust and evolving body of research to reference is key to our shared success.

Sharing knowledge

UX writers started building personal libraries, but that wasn't enough. We are people of words! We need to talk to one another. We need to collaborate out loud. So in 2020, Brain Traffic, the producer of Confab, a content strategy conference, held the first dedicated UXW conference, Button. Despite a global pandemic, economic hardship after national lockdowns, and significant political and social unrest in the United States, more than five hundred UXW and UXW-adjacent professionals came together online for three days to share experiences, discoveries, and novel research. It was the start of a more formal, cohesive community for global conversations about the direction of UXW. Among the live keynotes, fireside chats, Q&As, warm and lively Slack channels, on-demand library of prerecorded talks, breakout discussion groups, and social sessions—UX writers had found their home.

We need forums like Button not only for the ability to communicate the work we're doing as UX writers, but also for moral support and the efficiency of sharing what has been done before. Of course, we need to discuss these topics with those outside of our space, too. Whether that means giving internal presentations and workshops about UXW, showing results of copy tests for a specific touchpoint, or sharing processes, tools, and findings at conferences, we have to talk about what we do. Otherwise, we can't expect anyone to know about it.

And that's just the start. When we reach a new insight—that moment where it all clicks and we've synthesized everything we've read, seen, and heard about what others have experienced—the next step is to write it down. It doesn't matter if it's a tweet or a blog post, an internal memo or a report, an article in an industry newsletter, or a whole damn book. Sarah Winters (was Richards), who coined the term "content design" and authored a book of the same name, has encouraged the community to go the book route specifically. Don't say, "It's already been written." How many design and product books are out there? Is each and every one of them 100 percent unique? No. But do they each make a contribution, and is there infinite room for that in the field of UXW? Yes!

Don't say, "Who am I to write a book?" I'd challenge you by asking: Who are you to *not* write a book? If you have something to say, don't keep it from the rest of us. (Not cool.) We need to share our thoughts, experiences, and perspectives because we can all benefit from the diversity, fresh eyes, new angles, and evolving thoughts that build on what came before. Write a book. I did. I highly recommend it.

The next step

We've reached a time and place for deep introspection, which, in turn, has led to the course correction of our future as UX writers. Now that we're established and unified, it's time to have a think. Much of our journey and mission has been reactive. At this point, though, we should feel empowered to be proactive and to control our own fate. We've done a lot of good, even if a lot of it has been haphazard.

But where do we want to go next? We have the opportunity to slow down and be deliberate; I propose that we rethink our fanaticism about prioritizing the user at the expense of the business and start to think instead of users and businesses as each other's greatest advocates and partners.

The first step is course-correcting the overarching user-centeredness of UXW, which typically ignores the business as a partner in users' success. To do that, we need to harness our collective strength, optimize our knowledge sharing, leverage what others have already discovered, and align on the direction UXW needs to take now: bringing business considerations back to the core of UX optimization. As far as I know, this is the first book with that aim.

A note about who "we" are

We need to do the work. By "we," I mean people who do UXW, which includes many more people than carry the title of "UX writer." The most common titles for people who do UXW are UX writer and content designer, but there are many more, including (but not limited to): product writer, product content strategist, content strategist, UX content designer, and conversation designer.

At first, the field was so new that we had no idea what we wanted to be called. We did not know what people doing what we were doing were called at other organizations. And we did not fully understand the implications of what we called ourselves. Later, when we began to mature as a discipline, consensus started to form around "UX writer" to establish ourselves as product experts (as opposed to, say, marketing writers). Even later, this shifted to "content designer" as the need emerged to brand ourselves as designers, more than simply writers, of content.

There are many people who don't mind which title is used, or who see no real difference between them. Others feel strongly that the various titles are distinct and can't be used interchangeably.

Let's take a closer look at UX writers versus content designers, in terms of differences in scope:

- *UX writers* own the copy inside of the product: titles, subtitles, menus, pop ups, toasts, notifications, forms, empty states, error messages, and the like; and they write transactional emails and other touchpoints in user flows. They work with product managers to understand project specs and goals, and they work with designers to make things fit. They are first and foremost experts on the language in which they write—specifically grammar, colloquialisms, and vocabulary. They keep up to date on best practices and know their style guide by heart. They also, of course, know the ins and outs of their product and have a solid grasp of the space or industry the product lives in. They know all about their competitors' copy and understand business and user goals.
- *Content designers* are more focused on the structure of the content: how the copy appears on the page, progressive disclosure, and the informational relationships between different screens. They also, unsurprisingly, know a thing or two about design. They are not visual designers, but they have a solid grasp of visual design conventions. They specialize in hierarchy and navigation in a way that UX writers might not. (For a deep dive on that, I recommend *Writing is Designing* by Michael J. Metts and Andy Welfle.) They write like UX writers but also play a strategic design role.

I had an interesting conversation with Kristina Halvorson, CEO of Brain Traffic and founder of the Confab and Button conferences, in which we discussed the pros and cons of the terms "UX writer" and "content designer." I advocated for the former because I feel it's important to have "UX" in my title. This is because I want to:

- Make sure I'm always on the UX team, not the marketing or any other content team
- Come up in searches when recruiters on LinkedIn are specifically looking for UXers
- Be a part of mapping flows and journeys: UX, not just UI
- Have my opinions count when deciding on functionality: Should a user be able to cancel an upgrade within the product or only through customer support? What are the advantages and disadvantages of each option for the user and for the business?

But Halvorson advocated for the latter, not because she disagreed with what I was trying to frame through "UX," but because of the potential downside of calling myself a "writer," and because as soon as we are writers (as opposed to designers), we pigeonhole ourselves. We will only ever be asked about words—and not about content architecture, the best use of progressive disclosure, strategy, etc. We also might not get paid as much as our visual design counterparts.

She pointed to the early 2010s at Facebook, Shopify, and other tech giants, where "product content strategy" first emerged. From that point on, the idea of what we do was broken into three levels, described in an interview with Halvorson on the *Strings* blog:

Product content strategy is like the choreographer or the gatekeeper that oversees the function in the world of content, not only across product teams, but also making sure that voice, tone, messaging, the actual asset of the content as a product is in harmony with what's happening over [in] marketing, what's happening over in support, what's happening with technical content management, etc.

Content design is the set of activities that's very closely partnered with product strategy and design, thinking through requirements and features with a variety of stakeholders and users.

UX writing as a function is the actual "pen to paper." Where we are actually choosing the words. And this happens on the ground with active design, typically in sprints. (https://bkaprt. com/buxw43/01-06)

I still choose to use the label "UX writer," but regardless of the label you choose, we're all in this industry together—and that togetherness is where we'll see the most success.

UX WRITERS IN COLLABORATION

Tremendous personal growth comes from collaborating daily with engineers, designers, product managers, business stakeholders, and everyone else—the whole village. There is so much to learn from the experts we work with, and the perspectives they bring that are different than ours, while working toward the same goals.

Collaboration doesn't mean sharing a doc for the sake of iterating in the comments; it means sitting down and having a conversation about those comments—why they were made, what the context is, what should be considered when making a decision, where each stakeholder is coming from, how to align on the goal, and how to leverage what everyone has to offer, even when these offerings seem to be at odds with one another. These conversations can be mind-blowing—and the people you have them with are definitely worth getting to know. I can't tell you how much I've learned that has nothing to do with copy while collaborating on copy. Sometimes it seems like I should be paying to do my job instead of getting paid to do it. (Don't tell my boss.)

As fun and fulfilling as collaborating with interdisciplinary stakeholders can be, it also holds a critical, tactical function in highlighting the impact of UXW. Showing people the copy UX writers write is not enough to demonstrate what we can actually do.

It takes a village

Writing copy is only the first step in proving the positive impact of UXW. To complete the task, we need:

- **Engineers** to code data collection points in the product and set up tests
- **Data scientists** to analyze the data
- **Product managers** to schedule the work into sprints
- **Designers** to lay out the content, which makes up one moving part of the greater UX machine
- **Users**—at the research stage before and the analysis stage after—to give us guidance, because even when the numbers tell one story, the users can invalidate it

This is by no means a comprehensive list of collaborators, and it's certainly not a complete list of their contributions, but it should make clear how much of a team sport this all is.

When it comes to the business of UXW specifically, the most important village member we'll need to collaborate with is the business stakeholder. We'll need key business stakeholders to:

- **Confirm** that we are aiming toward a relevant goal
- **Validate** that we are measuring the most accurate, quantifiable proxies
- **Align** on the if-then hypothesis we start out with
- **Help** determine the actions we'll take, based on the results of our hypothesis
- **Advocate** for us to do more of this type of work in the future

Let's go back to our example of aiming to optimize the "Draw Funds" flow (**FIG. 1.3**).

The stakeholders *confirmed* that it was a top priority for the business. They *validated* the planned metrics—the number of draws and the overall utilization—as appropriate proxies for measuring achievement. They *aligned* on this hypothesis: "If we change the copy as follows, then users will draw more optimal amounts more frequently." Lastly, they *helped* determine that, were the metrics to back up the hypothesis, the test would be expanded to a larger test group. If the results scaled, they would *advocate* for the copy to be changed across the experience going forward.

The village came together. The business stakeholders confirmed, validated, aligned, helped, and advocated. Designers and UX writers crafted the exact variant(s) to test. Product managers scheduled the work into a sprint. Engineers coded the test. Data scientists set up the infrastructure for measuring the results and helped analyze them.

What's next? Say the test is successful, according to quantitative metrics and the if-then hypothesis. Users are drawing more optimal amounts from their accounts more frequently. We still need to validate these results with qualitative data. Why? Consider this scenario: you listen to recorded support calls and interview participants who completed the flow. Through this research, you discover that your solution reduced friction *so much* that users were clicking through the flow lightning fast, unable to process what they were agreeing to and ultimately needing the team to manually reverse the action. I think we can agree data like that would invalidate the previously defined "success."

Increasing draws in this case is not the ultimate goal; it's a means to an end. The ultimate goals are to increase business revenue and empower users to grow their own business through easy access to working capital. If users are drawing funds for the wrong reasons, that backfires for everyone. The business suffers from a damaged reputation and the cost of refunds. Users suffer because they're drawing more money than they can actually pay back, and they end up with delinquencies on their record and fees associated with bounced debits. An increase in numbers does not always equal success. Only when the whole village works together can true success happen, where everyone wins.

Create your local community

Being a part of a diverse village is awesome, but sometimes it can feel lonely to be the only UX writer in town. It's important for UX writers to get together in their own village, too.

FIG 1.5: There are all kinds of creative ways to make a community feel...communal. Team swag is one of my favorites.

We can start at home by creating a guild of writers within our organization. As the only UX writer at my company, my guild includes the marketing writer, corporate communications writers, the lead of sales (who supports content creation), the content strategist, and life cycle communications managers. Sometimes we invite product marketers who own messaging hierarchies, social media content creators, and brand managers to the party. We meet once a week, stay in touch in between with a dedicated Slack channel, and even made T-shirts (**FIG 1.5**). T-shirts are key.

Even though my everyday partners are designers, product managers, and engineers, I need my writing peeps close for brainstorming, troubleshooting, wordsmithing, naming conventions, content style guide maintenance and quality control, consistency across comms and journeys, and all that other good writing stuff.

Join the global community

Just like how Torrey Podmajersky collected UXW challenges at many companies and facilitated knowledge sharing by getting it all down in a book, Kristina Halvorson and Brain Traffic brought UX writers from around the world into the same (virtual) room for the first time at the annual Button conference to share their newest challenges, solutions, and innovations. Sarah Winters and Content Design London started—and still maintain—the crowd-sourced, evidence-based Readability Guidelines. Coming together as a global community expedites our collective learning and empowers us all to make a more significant impact on our products, from both a user and a business perspective.

We all need to look beyond our own organizations to build a coalition with other UX writers, in and outside of our industries. We each need to contribute to the local and global UXW communities, as well as to the communities in our products' spaces. These collaborations benefit us, our entire profession, our products and organizations, and society at large. It's why premier conferences like Button put such an emphasis on raising up new voices. The global community grows us as much as we grow the global community. There's no excuse not to get involved.

GETTING STARTED, IN A NUTSHELL

UXW has come a long way, and we should be proud of ourselves for creating something from nothing. We should be relieved that we are no longer lone soldiers, that we have like-minded practitioners *around the world* with whom we should be organizing—for the sake of companionship, but also for the sake of sharing knowledge and innovations in our field. We have advocates in other departments, too, who understand what we can do to make them more successful. A big part of this will involve working with business stakeholders to leverage organically aligned user and business interests. To do this, we all need to get better acquainted.

WHERE UX WRITING AND BUSINESS MEET

ALL THIS TALK ABOUT UX writers supporting business goals begs the question: How is a UX writer meant to identify business goals in the first place? It's not the kind of information we learn in a UXW bootcamp, and it was not likely part of our orientation when we joined the design team (though it probably should've been). Assuming we're all on the same page now about how important it is for UX writers to understand business goals, we need a path to get there.

GETTING TO KNOW YOUR BUSINESS PARTNER

Let's start by identifying the source of the problem. Here are some reasons why UX writers might not be looped into business goals right off the bat:

- No one thought the writer would be interested.
- These goals might not actually exist.
- These goals might exist, but only in the founder's head.

Accessible, up-to-date documentation on goals with executive consensus is, unfortunately, not the norm. So the UX writer who wants to use UXW to support business goals has to start by articulating those goals, whether that means finding them or asking the business to put them down on paper for the first time, or the first time in a while, in some form or another.

Collect and document the business's goals

There are a few ways to go about collecting and documenting business goals. First, we can identify if documentation already exists. Ask managers, peers, and any colleagues who have been at the company for a long time and who have historical context. Not every UX writer will feel like they have easy access to executives or have much visibility into documentation that was created before they arrived on the scene, but we all have access to peers and teammates. Some of us may be able to reach out directly to higher-ups, while others might ask our manager to escalate our inquiry. No matter where we sit in the organization, we should be able to identify the organization's documented goals if we are proactive about it.

If there are documented goals, great. We need to review the documentation, whether that's a Google Doc, a Confluence page, a PowerPoint presentation, or some other format. We need to start thinking about which of those goals we might be able to impact with UXW and create focused priorities for our own work. We also need to note the time frames and metrics that already accompany these high-level goals.

Next, we need to organize our targets by goals and subgoals, and then categorize them into short, medium, and long-term. We should show our final documentation—where we've synthesized and organized business goals through a UXW lens—to our higher-ups, gaining feedback and context on the greater product roadmap. That way, we can start planning the most strategic methods and moments to make our contributions. Managers should also be able to provide insight into how business stakeholders are measuring success so that we can get aligned—because it's critical to know how to prove our success and to whom.

Finally, we need to formalize a way to track progress—things we tried that worked or didn't—by gaining insight from lessons we learned and remembering them for the future. Ideally, this will be a living, dynamic document that we can easily update and share over time.

Develop goals

If goals do not exist in a meaningful way, we can jump-start their development by creating documentation. The format doesn't matter, as long as it's simple and lends itself well to updates and collaboration (think Google Docs, Google Sheets, Google Slides). It might sound unrealistic for a UX writer to develop organization-wide goals, but do not despair! The objective of articulating business goals is to provide a framework for success in our own work in a way that's also meaningful to the business. I'm not saying every business goal should apply to every discipline across the organization. What's needed is documentation that gives us something to aim for, keeps business interests top of mind as we work, and provides guardrails and signposts for our UXW.

It's okay to make educated guesses, because even if we don't get it right the first time, having something down on paper is still helpful. It's also great for getting feedback from people— even if it's just to say how wrong we are—which also gets the conversation going. Long story short, we need a North Star to follow. Some UX writers may have a greater hand in defining this North Star business goal, while others may have it mostly prescribed. Both need it on their desks before they write a single word.

Each goal we document needs a definition of success to go with it. The North Star gives us a direction to aim for; success metrics let us know how close we're getting. Again, it doesn't really matter if we're not able to get confirmed North Stars from day one. So long as we have a goal—any goal—to work toward, and against which we can track our progress, our work will not have been wasted. Even if we got it all wrong and are then corrected, we:

GOAL + Def. of Success

- **Got the attention** of the stakeholders who were needed to set up the goal posts that we couldn't get clear definitions for earlier
- **Demonstrated** that UXW can move the needle (even if, this time, it was the wrong needle)

Approve goals

Whatever our documented business goals look like—whether they were preexisting or compiled by yours truly, whether comprehensive and official or a best guess just for the sake of getting started—it helps to get some validation before beginning. We need some kind of confirmation that resources will be allocated for pursuing the goals we've laid out, and that the metric(s) we plan to use as proxies for success will be considered credible evidence of our impact.

Getting goals approved also means we've invited and confirmed visibility into our work. Transparency prevents surprises. We definitely do not want to find ourselves in the position of surprising business stakeholders with a massive UXW project we've invested in, only to be told that in their eyes, we've wasted extensive resources. Or, we don't want to discover that we've invested resources in a worthwhile goal but measured the wrong metric, so actually we have no idea whether we've succeeded according to the business.

If business stakeholders have visibility into what we're planning to do, everyone can get aligned early, increasing the likelihood of consensus later. Once we have results, we won't have to waste time and energy explaining why we did what we did. We can skip to the part where we assess the outcomes and determine next steps as a team.

Surprises are also bad because they frame the relationship between UX writers and business stakeholders as "us" versus "them," instead of as a cohesive team with common goals. As UX writers, we create work that we present to stakeholders; we provide opinions and they give feedback. By not surprising "them," by being transparent, and ideally by engaging them and authentically being interested in their insights from the beginning, everyone involved has a sense of ownership. Everyone automatically feels better about and more invested in a project that is theirs. Work together from day one, and you have more talented people who bring more to the table and who care about mutual success. After all, we're all in it together.

Set responsible goals

Until now, we've taken the value of business goals as a given, striving to achieve the goals that have been set. But we skipped a step, and that is to take responsibility—as the intermediary between the business and the users, and as the user advocate internally—and think critically about whether our goals are ethical. First, *pause*. Drop the documentation; take a step (or two) back. Ask yourself: Are these goals that *should* be pursued? Are they the right thing to strive for, ethically?

Ethics are not simple, and in a lot of ways, technological advances have made them all the more complicated. Say a business goal is to increase session time. What does this goal give back to users? Is it helping them curb an unhealthy addiction? Great—the goal seems ethical and aligned. Is it distracting them from being attentive at their kid's soccer game? We may need to think twice about that one. Even if, technically, the business generates more revenue the longer a user stays in-app—shopping, let's say—and the user also wants to spend more time in-app because they've come there specifically for a leisurely shopping experience, is session time still an ethical metric? What user research do we have that may shed light on the real-world implications of session time on users, their families, or their communities?

The takeaway here is not some soapbox speech about how people should be spending their time and the role of tech companies in curbing free will. It's a cry for us to take ownership over the ethics of how we communicate with users, and to act as gatekeepers when need be, taking business goals off the table if and when they harm our users. Protecting the moral fiber of our app is certainly in our business's and our users' best interests, as abstract and intangible as that might seem. If that's a hard case to make at your company, it might be time to find a new job.

What if you feel like a small fish in your large organization? You may feel that this section doesn't apply to you. Who are you to be an ethics gatekeeper? To be clear: ethical responsibility applies to all of us. You may just have to make your case louder. It may be riskier and less comfortable for you personally, but at the end of the day, we're human before we're writers, and we have a responsibility to advocate for a more ethical society. Even small tweaks—like choosing to write "blocklist" or simply "list" instead of "blacklist," which associates being Black with being bad and white with being good—are something we all should be able to do, inching us toward a more equitable world, which will positively impact every single person, user, product, and business.

Okay. Now that our goals are set, how do we go about attacking them? It's time to make an impact.

KAPOW!

Once we have a sufficient grasp of the business's goals overall, it's time to apply a UXW lens. We need to decide which goals to focus on, propose solutions, and prioritize which potential solutions to try first.

This is where having a *UX writing framework* to maximize ROI comes into play. The acronym KAPOW can help remind you how to maximize impact (**FIG 2.1**):

- Know your goals
- Articulate solutions
- Prioritize options
- Own your metrics
- Write

For the rest of this chapter, we'll break down each step and include a real-world example. (While generally based on real work I've done, some details will be oversimplified, exaggerated, or otherwise changed to better illustrate the points being made. These examples don't necessarily reflect the opinions or goals of any company.)

KAPOW *'s GOAL : Max. ROI from UXW*

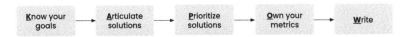

| Know your goals | → | Articulate solutions | → | Prioritize solutions | → | Own your metrics | → | Write |

FIG 2.1: KAPOW is a framework for maximizing the ROI of UXW.

Know your goals

Now that we have a list of goals, let's remove those where UXW is not a (significant) factor and keep those that UXW can impact in a meaningful way.

For example, I'm working on a product that offers credit to small businesses. The core happy flow consists of users:

1. Applying for credit
2. Being approved for credit
3. Landing on a dashboard where they can draw funds from their credit lines
4. Repaying funds they've borrowed, and then borrowing funds again

One goal is to reduce drop-off in the application part of the flow, in other words, to increase the number of applicants who finish the application.

Another goal is optimal borrowing, measured in a number of ways, including:

- Time from approval to first draw
- Frequency of draws
- Total utilization

There is a lot of room for UXW to impact the goal of reducing drop-off, either by motivating users or by removing technical barriers for users throughout the application. This business goal should stay on the list.

However, user approval is not up to us. It's much less dependent on UXW and more about the creditworthiness of the users, the specific users that marketing drives to apply, the underwriting models, and other factors. This business goal should not stay on our list.

Sometimes, the decision about whether a goal should or shouldn't stay on our list won't be that obvious. Consider goals around how users borrow funds. UXW can motivate users to draw optimal amounts and remove technical barriers by making it clear how to use the feature. But what if those are not the barriers to entry? What if users are already motivated and already understand exactly what to do but feel that the fees are too high? UXW can't fix that. Perhaps we could better explain why the fees are what they are or in some other way express empathy for this user hesitation, but the potential ROI for UXW here is relatively low. You might need to do a little research to be confident, though, about whether to leave it on the list or take it off.

Next, it's time to prioritize the short list, because we won't be able to attack all the goals at once. It's a good sign if the company has more ambition than resources, but it's not an excuse to sacrifice sleep and stretch resources further until burnout takes over. The solution is to prioritize. To do that, we can take inspiration from the RICE framework often used in product management.

RICE stands for *Reach, Impact, Confidence,* and *Effort.*

Reach

We can start by assessing each of the goals and asking ourselves what the reach is, meaning: How many users will see the copy we write? Let's compare the reach of UXW in the context of two business goals: increasing draws on a credit line and decreasing draws that are repaid early. The former has much greater reach because, if we're doing things right, many users are drawing funds regularly, while far fewer are repaying early. Therefore, copy in the Draw Funds flow will have greater reach than copy in the Repay Early flow. This reach assessment may mean prioritizing the Draw Funds flow over the Repay Early flow, but there are additional factors to take into consideration as well. Just because more users will see the copy doesn't mean it'll have more impact.

Impact

In addition to reach, we should assess how much impact the copy may have on users. In the example above, copy in the Draw Funds flow will have high reach, but will it have high impact? How likely is it that we'll write copy that significantly increases draws? We'll get more eyes on the copy, but will the copy affect change in the users who see it? Try to home in on goals with UXW potential for high reach *and* high impact.

home or hone?

If the flow's friction is due to users misunderstanding how to draw funds, there is enormous potential for UXW to make an impact. However, if the friction is due to the fee rate—as we considered earlier—it's a different story. UXW might be able to help a little by explaining the rate so that users feel more comfortable, but at the end of the day, copy is not going to bring down the rate and may not have much impact on the overall goal, despite its far reach.

Now consider the potential impact of UXW on the lower-reach Repay Early flow. It's easier to convince someone to keep their money, instead of paying off a debt early, than it is to convince someone to pay a fee to borrow funds. Impact is likely to be higher when the goal is easier. For this goal, the reach is lower, but the potential impact is higher—so how do we prioritize the two? Where do we start, and how much do we invest in each?

None of this is clear-cut or completely objective. This framework is not meant to be an algorithm where we feed in goals, and out pop answers about how to prioritize our UXW roadmap. A framework is a way of thinking about our work. We may be able to quantify reach, but we're unlikely to get a hard number to measure impact, and it gets even more complicated when considering our level of confidence in our own estimations.

Confidence

Confidence is equally important to our assessments of reach and impact, and should be factored into our prioritization. Continuing with the Draw Funds and Repay Early flow examples, we have high confidence in our reach assessment because we can see in the quantitative data exactly how many users get to the relevant screens. However, we're apt to be less confident about our assessment of potential impact because our assumptions are probably not based on concrete data.

One way to increase confidence in impact is by talking to users. Perhaps, in the Draw Funds flow, we've assumed that the barrier to entry is high fees; therefore, we don't see a lot of potential for UXW to have an impact. But what if the barrier is a hesitation about the transfer of funds? (How secure is the transfer? How much time does it take?) If that's the case, we can use UXW to explain those barriers away. Talking to users in this case can help increase confidence in our impact assessment and help us accurately prioritize goals. It doesn't take a *lot* of research, but *Just Enough Research*—which also happens to be the name of a book by Erika Hall that I highly recommend reading.

Doing just enough research will slightly increase the scope of the effort (which is the last element in RICE), but it'll save a lot more effort than it would cost if we were to skip it, build the wrong solution, and end up back at the beginning.

Effort

Lastly, we need to consider the effort required to address each goal on the list. For each goal, how much writing, design, development, product, legal, and other resources would be required to create, implement, measure, and analyze the success (or failure) of the UXW solutions?

Whenever possible, we also need to take into consideration dependencies, like whether we can or can't complete a copy task until decisions come back from outside legal counsel; or whether we can't QA our work until our emailing system gets through sending a big batch of emails from a different task; or

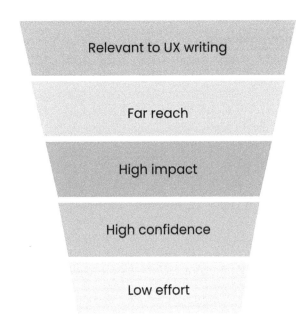

Relevant to UX writing

Far reach

High impact

High confidence

Low effort

FIG 2.2: We can work through a funnel to narrow our goals, starting with all the possible goals we can aim to achieve, and ending with a focused group of goals to start working on now.

even whether certain stakeholders who must sign off on the final copy are on vacation. Dependencies can't always be predicted, and even those we anticipate can't necessarily be sized accurately. So, we just need to be aware that dependences will affect the scope of the effort for each solution, without expecting to define this factor accurately.

At the end of the RICE assessment, we should know our goals and be able to illustrate them in a funnel (**FIG 2.2**).

We started with a broad list of business goals, filtered them through a UXW lens, and prioritized them by reach, impact, confidence, and effort. Now we really know our goals—and, hopefully, already have a few potential solutions floating around in our brains. The next step is getting those solutions out of our heads, refining them, and sharing them with the team.

Articulate solutions

Research should guide our decisions about which solutions to try first. It's not about choosing which feels the most elegant to us, which would be easiest to implement, or any number of other factors. Those considerations will all weigh in eventually, of course, but step one is to make an evidence-based choice about the direction to pursue.

Understand the barrier

In the example above, we had several hypotheses about the barriers to business goals. Was the real friction in the Draw Funds flow about fee rates, transfer details, understanding (on a technical level) how to complete the flow, or something else entirely? It's best not to articulate solutions until after we narrow down exactly what we're solving for.

User research comes before all of the writing. Find out how users use the product, and why; what's working, and what isn't; what they understand, and where they need help; what language resonates, and what alienates. This information is fundamental to doing our job well—and often intrigues—because writing for a digital product is not like writing a poem or a book, where success is more or less in the eye of the beholder. When we write in UI, it's not for us, and it's not to be judged subjectively. UI writing is "good" when it works, and to achieve that, we need to start from data. Tools like FullStory (https://bkaprt.com/buxw43/02-01) and UserTesting (https://bkaprt.com/buxw43/02-02) make research more accessible, but simple interviews and support / sales call recordings will do the trick, too.

This isn't a one-time thing, either. We should be testing almost everything we do. Unlike many other forms of writing, our work is not done once we publish; in fact, publishing means we're only about halfway there. The next step is to track our copy's performance and plan the next iteration. This part can be exhilarating, providing proof that there are real live people interacting with *our* words to accomplish things. But not always.

I can't say I love surprisingly disappointing results, like button copy I assumed would double engagement but actually had no effect at all; or the email subject line that was rewritten for compliance purposes and not expected to affect open rates—but ended up slashing opens in half. But even in those cases, it felt good to know we were following up and making tweaks where necessary to do right by our users, even if it took a spoonful of humility.

Identify the lowest-hanging fruit

Say we've done enough qualitative user research to determine that fees are not the problem; rather, it's users' understanding of how to draw funds. A logical next step would be to dig into existing quantitative metrics. If there are three steps in the Draw Funds flow, we might look at how many users are dropping off at each step. We may be able to articulate solutions to optimize each step, but we'd want to prioritize the solution with the most to gain—in this case, the step with the highest drop-off is where we have the most to gain from investing in UXW.

Get inspired through market research

Feeling stuck? It might help to take a look at how other businesses have already solved for the problems we've prioritized. Of course, we'd need to extrapolate which elements of their solutions apply to our business and which are less relevant.

In the case of the Draw Funds flow, where we've determined that the primary obstacle is understanding how to draw—specifically during the first step, where the user chooses an amount to draw—we'd look at copy at that touchpoint in competitors' products, likely gaining some useful insights:

- Maybe they offer a chatbot at that point to advise users on how much to draw.
- Maybe they prepopulate a suggested amount, to lower users' cognitive load and remove the friction of typing a number.
- Maybe they offer a few prepopulated options to allow users to feel in control by choosing their own amount while also having the option not to type anything.

- Maybe they have dynamic helper text that provides personalized advice based on users' past draws.

We can use all of these ideas to inspire UXW solutions that make sense for our product. I'm not suggesting copying other businesses' solutions—we know our own users best, and our users are always different than our competitors' in some way—but others' solutions can be a great source of inspiration as we figure out what might work for us.

Prioritize solutions

Next, we need to take the solutions we've articulated and prioritize them. We probably have a few great ideas at this point, and likely more solutions than we'll be able to test all at once.

Curate a short list

Write down the pros and cons of each potential solution, and then bounce them off relevant stakeholders. It's not rare to end up pursuing a hybrid of a few solutions.

Beware: this isn't the time or place to fall in love with your work. Know ahead of time that you're preparing a "solution brain dump" where one winner will emerge, with all the rest falling to the wayside. Having a high quantity of solutions is an important first step in reaching a high-quality solution, so try not to be precious about any one idea.

Bouncing solutions off stakeholders is good for more than collecting opinions; it can also uncover limitations, such as engineering bandwidth. The latter is particularly important for adjusting the dependencies and overall effort estimation from the RICE assessment. There's a chance that, after understanding the effort involved in implementing and testing proposed solutions, we may decide to pivot and work on a different goal altogether. That's okay. Better to catch it now, before investing even more in a project with a potentially low ROI. Accepting sunk costs and knowing when to cut losses is part of how this works. Edit your list until you have a set of solutions that are supported by user research, inspired by market research, and

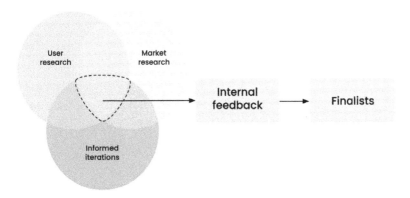

FIG 2.3: Once we've defined our goals and challenges, it's time to narrow down the many creative solutions we've come up with to discover the ones worth testing first.

iterated and improved as new information is discovered. Run that set by your stakeholders to help you arrive at a subset of finalists (**FIG 2.3**).

Implement solution #1

Assuming we don't work at a huge organization—with the resources (development bandwidth, users, etc.) to test each solution finalist simultaneously—we'll need to pick one solution to start with. The hope is we succeed early, removing the need to go through every solution we articulated, but that's a consideration for later. For now, let's implement solution #1.

Think laterally across all of the goals

Up until this point, we've been talking about solutions for a single goal, but it's more likely that you'd be solving for multiple goals at once. Regardless of whether you're a lone soldier or part of a bigger team, and especially if you're a manager, you're going to need to think laterally across all goals while choosing the best way forward for each.

But it's not enough to prioritize your own solutions to your own goals. After choosing which solution to test first—knowing it might fail, in which case you'll move on to your second choice—you need to prioritize these tests against other engineering tasks in the sprint. This is done in collaboration with product managers; you may even need to convince them why they should remove a different task to make room for yours.

Don't forget: there's always opportunity cost at play. Every time the team works on something, it means they're not working on something else. It's important to know—and to be able to explain, inside and out—why a UXW task is more valuable to the business than whatever else will not get done while the team works on it.

Joshua Arnold's Cost of Delay concept (https://bkaprt.com/buxw43/02-03) can help you have an effective conversation with the product manager. Consider talking about how much value the copy would be contributing if it existed now, versus if it got implemented soon, versus if it were pushed to later. What's the opportunity cost of *not* prioritizing the UXW task? Instead of making a case for why we need what we need, we're talking about how they (product managers) can't live without it. That's powerful.

Own your metrics

Without metrics, it's nearly impossible to know whether we've just made things better, made them worse, or had no impact at all. It's also difficult to understand the ROI of the UXW work. By showing us not only whether something worked, but also why, metrics shed light on how to make our solutions even more powerful.

Define success

You should know from the beginning exactly what success looks like for your solution. Here are a few suggestions for defining this:

- **Use if-then statements.** We've all heard the saying that the practice of statistics is (at least) as much art as it is science. I've seen it myself where a content person runs a test, brings forward data making it clear that they'd proved or disproved a hypothesis, and was then told by the stakeholder to whom they presented the data that in fact, the data supports the exact opposite hypothesis. Two people looked at the same data, the same numbers, the same "proof," and reached conflicting conclusions. To avoid this situation, it's critical to start with if-then statements. Using our earlier goal in the Draw Funds flow, we might use the statement, "If 5 percent more users in the test group draw funds in their first seven days, then the copy was successful." That way, when we bring out the data at the end of the experiment, everyone will be aligned on how to interpret it and whether to define the test as a success or not.

- **Do not write if-then statements on your own.** Regardless of whom you report your findings to at the end, they'll need to buy in to how you define success. Together, you should imagine the possible outcomes of the copy test and agree ahead of time on what each outcome will mean.

  Say we were about to use the if-then statement mentioned earlier. It may have sounded pretty straightforward to us, but then we brought it to a business stakeholder who said, "Yeah, more users drawing in their first week is good, but what if they start drawing a lower amount overall?" Together, we might modify our if-then statement to: "If 5 percent more users draw in their first seven days after approval, and if their overall utilization is above 50 percent over their first month after approval, then the copy was successful." If we'd moved ahead with the statement we'd formulated on our own, we never would have measured utilization, and our results wouldn't have gotten us very far. Throughout all of this, it's critical to document. We've defeated the whole point of aligning at the beginning if alignment can be sabotaged by selective memory at the end.
- **Define endpoints.** Before getting started, define when the test will be over. The test may last a certain amount of time or run until a certain number of users have joined each group (test and control). Whatever the endpoint, align on it beforehand to avoid bringing data at the end, only to be

told: "Sure, but that's not enough data to draw conclusions. It doesn't count until..."

- **Layer metrics.** Human behavior is rarely simple, so to draw meaningful conclusions about copy's effect on users' behaviors, layer a few metrics on top of one another. More about this in Chapter 4.
- **Factor in the cost of the test.** Tests themselves have costs, for example, engineering, analysis, and participant recruitment. When crunching the numbers around ROI, it's important to include the test's overhead as part of the investment side of the equation.

We'll dive deeper into metrics in Chapter 4, but for the KAPOW framework, it's important to embrace our ownership of this part of UXW as the UX writers. We don't need to be the best UX researcher in the room or the most mathematically astute analyst. But we do need to take responsibility for establishing what "success" means, and aligning stakeholders on that meaning, before a copy test begins—which includes pulling in the right partners when writing out if-then statements, defining endpoints, layering metrics to get more robust results, and reminding the team to factor in the cost of the test itself.

Recycle, reuse

Once success has been defined, it's time to measure it. I highly recommend inventorying current measurements before scoping out new ones. "How am I supposed to know that technical stuff?" you ask. You're not. But you are supposed to find out about it. What measurements are already being taken that might apply to our test? What data is being collected through Google Analytics or other platforms that we can leverage? Use what you've got; everyone loves free metrics.

But there's another side to this coin. We shouldn't feel limited to using out-of-the-box metrics. Sometimes custom metrics will need to be implemented, and that's okay. If no existing metrics are applicable for our test at all, that's also okay—so long as we've confirmed it before moving on. It might take a combination of measurements to validate findings, both quantitative and qualitative.

In an episode of the *NN/g UX Podcast,* Nielsen Norman Group director Kate Moran acknowledged that ROI may be overwhelming at first to UX writers who aren't coming from a background that includes a lot of math (https://bkaprt.com/buxw43/02-04). That said—as she wrote in an article posted to the Nielsen Norman Group website—communicating the value of UX is not always about exact numbers (https://bkaprt.com/buxw43/02-05). It can also be a thought exercise, introducing a useful lens that helps writers and designers think about their work in a business-oriented way, and that helps business stakeholders consider UXW a business imperative and not a nice-to-have. Talking in the language of "this copy change will be good for our bottom line" with exact numbers is a significant bridge between departments that can pave the way for collaboration useful to the business and its users.

It's good to be wrong sometimes, because it means that we can be confident in the times that we're right—we're really right. Multiple techniques exist to help protect the integrity of your data. Here are two:

- **Recruit carefully:** Even before getting in a room with users, know that we are all susceptible to bias during the recruitment process. Be mindful of whether you are profiling participants and inviting those most likely to support your hypothesis. My favorite example of this was in a cartoon showing that 100 percent of survey participants like taking surveys. Hm, think about it.
- **Outsource:** Have someone neutral gather and assess the data without telling them your hypothesis. Get them in a room with users and let them walk away with their own impressions, with no idea which answer you were rooting for.

It's impossible to eliminate bias completely, but we can somewhat mitigate the potential for bias by keeping it top of mind, using mixed methods for better validation, collaborating with neutral partners, and collecting enough data to separate real trends from artifacts.

There is no *M* in KAPOW for metrics; there's an *O* for ownership because it's easy to think that metrics are for "numbers people," not "words people" like us. But it's on us to take ownership over metrics measuring the ROI of UXW. We're not expected to build Tableau tables—of course not—but we should be expected to manage the process, liaise between relevant parties, ask all the questions, and empower the collaborators and partners who are as desperately eager as we are to find reliable results to accurately assess solutions.

Write

Finally! Who knew there was so much for a UX writer to do before writing? The truth is, before we reach this stage, we have already started writing.

- We wrote lists of goals, and then sublists, and then sublists of sublists.
- We drafted solutions.
- We wrote decks to present the tests to various stakeholders.

Now it's time to finalize the actual words that will be going into the product—starting from the solution drafts. We should mostly be on polishing duty: double-checking that we've aligned with best practices and heuristics, product voice, tone, and style, and the rest of the existing product experience. We should also get approvals on the final copy from the compliance and legal departments, and anyone else who is part of the process. Dot all the i's and cross all the t's; it's time to go live.

Microcopy is the tip of an iceberg. *K, A, P,* and *O* all come first and buoy the actual writing above the surface for all to see. Diving into everything that goes into the actual writing is for a different book (or several). When it comes to the ROI of UXW, what's important is that many major steps—which are also the UX writers' job—come before the writing, and that product copy is far from the only words we write.

Once the copy is live and the test results are in, we'll also write up one last document summarizing the project, the outcomes, and the informed action items. Every bit of this is critical for UX writers, our field, the business's long-term success, and, most importantly, the users.

GETTING UNDER THE HOOD

The meeting point between business and UXW is clearest once we look under the hoods of each for similarities. Once we dig into understanding what each can contribute, and once we appreciate the overlap in our respective goals, working together could not be more natural. That doesn't mean we don't still need processes and frameworks. KAPOW is a framework based on a business lens, which makes clear to business stakeholders how their considerations are our considerations. The next level of getting under the hood is not just breaking down our process, but truly understanding why it works.

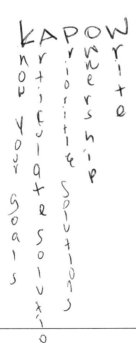

3 HOW UX WRITING INCREASES ROI

TO REFRESH, THE RETURN on investment (ROI) is the amount of money an organization makes compared to the amount it spends to make it. If, for example, a business spends one million dollars to make one million dollars, the ROI is not good. They've spent everything they've made! That business is not profitable, even though they've just made a million dollars. Naturally, the higher the ROI, the better. Kate Moran described ROI as the bridge between metrics and key performance indicators (KPIs), which reflect business goals and indicate whether the organization is meeting those goals in a numeric way (https://bkaprt.com/buxw43/03-01).

There are two ways to improve ROI: by increasing return and by decreasing investment. In other words, to increase our profit, we need to increase revenue or decrease costs. In the case of UXW, I suggest we invest a little, return a lot, and save on expenses, too. The reason UXW is a great place to invest a little—and why doing so will pay off a lot—is because changing the copy in a product is relatively inexpensive.

My favorite example comes from Jared Spool, who worked for an organization that decided that users, in the middle of their checkout flow, would be required to register on the site.

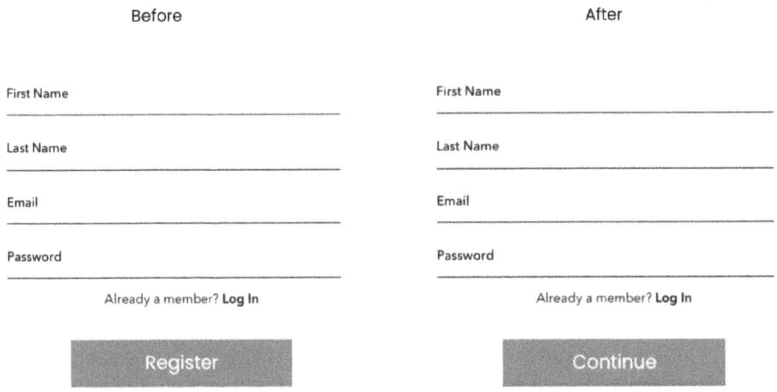

Before

After

First Name

First Name

Last Name

Last Name

Email

Email

Password

Password

Already a member? **Log In**

Already a member? **Log In**

Register

Continue

FIG 3.1: These illustrations show how a one-word copy change from "Register" (left) to "Continue" (right) increased revenue by 300 million dollars.

I'm sure the UXers who were given such a requirement (adding a registration form to the middle of an ecommerce purchase flow) pushed back. But the decision was made, and the button copy at the end of the registration step was to be "Register." Makes sense. But the users did not want to register. They wanted to continue making their purchase. So, the button copy was changed from "Register" to "Continue," which resulted in 45 percent more users completing the purchase flow (**FIG 3.1**). This equaled 15 million dollars more in sales during the first month and 300 million dollars more in sales during the first year—success that came after the button copy was changed (https://bkaprt.com/buxw43/03-02).

Changing that button copy may not have been the only solution to increase ROI here, but it was a particularly effective one because it was so cheap. In other scenarios, the cost-benefit analysis may not be as easy to predict, so UX writers may propose multiple solutions: some may be copy-based and therefore very cheap; some may involve design tweaks and therefore cost a little more; and some may even require more expensive work on the backend. In a healthy company, it should be completely natural for the UX writer to ask engineers to provide estimates for different solutions. It's fully within any UX writer's scope— together with the designer—to judge the relative impact on the user experience when comparing cheaper and more expensive solutions. Any product manager should be thrilled to have their UX writers thinking about saving business resources and reaching out to engineers to gather the necessary numbers and research.

GET A SEAT AT THE TABLE

To do cost-benefit analyses, it's not just engineers we'll need to talk to. Any conversation about ROI is going to involve business stakeholders, so we need to be sitting at the same table.

UX writers in different organizations may be looking for seats at different tables. Some may have their eye on the mahogany table in the boardroom with the business stakeholders who determine the direction of the product on a high level, while others are eyeing the picnic table with their local product manager and designer. Either way, the table is where the fundamentals are decided, where context is built, and where involvement means exponential impact on the final deliverable. We UX writers complain about being brought in at the last minute, when the business goal that the feature is aiming for has already been finalized, the functionality fully defined, the metrics for success decided on and in place, and the pixel-perfect designs sitting with empty containers for us to fill with words. We want to be involved at an earlier stage—before everyone got up from the table and down to work—and talking business can get us there.

For a long time, the UXW community has been on the defensive, justifying why we do what we do, and explaining why investing in our work adds to the business (as opposed to taking away from it). If the best defense is offense, we find ourselves aggressively shouting or begging to be included at the table early and often, to be given the autonomy to make decisions, and to be allowed more resources. We find ourselves in an "us versus them" paradigm, where *they* have built a wall of exclusivity that *we* need to bust through. But wouldn't it be better if our presence was invited and not forced? Things would be way more pleasant. We'd also increase the likelihood of getting a real say and not just a performative seat at the table. Inclusion doesn't mean another representative face in the room instead of outside the door; it means speaking and being heard.

As UX writers, we understand the importance of knowing our audience and speaking their language in order to connect. In this case, business stakeholders are the audience, and our message will be best received if it's delivered in terms they care about. We don't need our stakeholders to understand everything we do, just as we will never understand everything they do. What's important is to focus on the intersection of what we each do, finding the synergy of both our skill sets and maximizing the benefit to both the user and the business.

Help me help you

I want to highlight a complementary approach presented by Greta van der Merwe at Confab 2021 (https://bkaprt.com/buxw43/03-03). She suggested shifting our focus from *when* we're being included to what we can do *once* we're included—whenever that is. Instead of saying, "Bring me in early so I can do *A*!" say: "If you bring me in early, I can do *A*; if you bring me in later, I can do *B*. Which do you want, *A* or *B*?" This changes the perceived reason for our asking to be included: it's no longer because *we* want it, rather it's for the business to get more out of it.

Here's an example of what van der Merwe means. Once, on a complicated financial product my team was working on, I, the UX writer, was brought in before a single low-fidelity wireframe existed. I was able to contribute to the content hierarchy, applying my specialized knowledge about what and how users read—and in turn, where and how to include the various pieces of content. Had I been brought in later, I would've written clear, concise, and helpful words, but they would not have been structured to best delight the user and motivate them to do what the business would like them to do (and what they came to the product to do).

I was also able to champion users' perspectives about what content was most valuable. The business decided to offer two repayment plan options, but I was brought in early enough to make the case for whether, where, and how to show the exact dates and amounts for each repayment. Other stakeholders had the same information that I had, but I had the skill set and expertise to recommend the best copy for the flow. When the business gets to see that, the business wants UX writers at the table early. I've even been brought in so early that there was no real way for me to contribute yet! But I'd rather the invitation overshoot in that direction, if it were up to me.

I've worked with my product managers, designers, and business stakeholders long enough that they invite me to join them early on; I don't need to invite myself. They understand that bringing me in early gets them *A* and bringing me in later gets them *B*, and they very much want *A*. Getting to this point can be a process. It's important to stay calm and remember that, at the end of the day, we all have the same goals—serving the users and the business. We need to assume good intent and know that if we're not invited, it's not an intentional slight or a belittling of what we can contribute, but a lack of understanding.

This approach goes a long way toward minimizing frustration and misunderstandings on both sides. Because we're not locked into delivering whatever's possible when we're brought in late, we're not judged on work we know could have been better. The business also gets the maximum of what we have to offer. There's always potential for UXW, but they need to help us help them. This approach frames our roles as a partnership and deep collaboration, which will always be more productive than standing on a soap box.

Close the gap

To clarify, when UX writers ask to be pulled into the conversation early and often, it's not coming from a place of ego or self-righteousness. Not at all. We're advocating for a bigger role because we know that the bigger our role, the greater our impact. When we're given resources and autonomy, and when roles and responsibilities are broad, deep, and well established, both businesses and users benefit.

However, while we want to make our contribution, like everyone else who is invested in the business's success, we find ourselves running into unique obstacles that other contributors

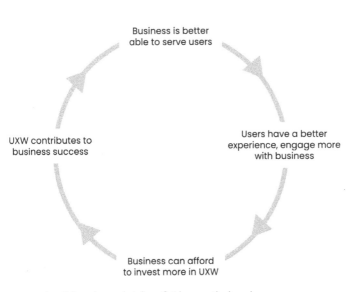

Business is better
able to serve users

UXW contributes to
business success

Users have a better
experience, engage more
with business

Business can afford
to invest more in UXW

FIG 3.2: A collaborative cycle is beneficial across the board.

may not. In my opinion, many of those barriers are created or perpetuated by a disconnect between what we know and what the business decision-makers know. We can close that gap by speaking their language, the language of dollars and cents.

If we can use our tool kit to save business-development costs on one feature, that money can be reallocated to serve users with new features. If we help the business save in customer-support costs, they can invest in more sophisticated user-support tools, leveling up our users' overall support experience. When the business invests in UXW, UXW invests in the business. This positive feedback cycle benefits everyone, not least of all our users (**FIG 3.2**).

Once upon a time, at a company where I worked, transactional emails were a mess. Their look and feel were inconsistent because each one was being designed and developed individually. That meant a lot of resources were going into creating and maintaining a bad user experience. Streamlining our emails would mean less design time and less development time—great for the business, which could now design and develop other things without adding investment overall—while giving users a better email experience.

When I say we needed a new email design system, I don't mean visually, though of course that was a core part of the restructuring. The reason UXW led this effort is because emails are one place where I do believe in a content-first approach. And so the focus became information architecture: what kinds of content blocks would we need?

I started by consulting the engineering team to understand the technical considerations for creating an email-specific content design system. My initial ask was for a completely modular system where I had a wide library of content chunks that I could shuffle around however I wanted, for each email. Engineering's preference was for a limited set of static templates that I would choose from and force content into each time. Neither was going to work.

What we settled on was a collection of templates, each containing a finite set of content blocks that I could write or nullify—but could not add to or change the order of—each time. It was a perfect cross between engineering considerations (avoiding a completely modular system) and content considerations (allowing for a wide variety of content structures to optimize the content consumption of different email communications) (FIG 3.3).

By using various combinations of elements from the same base template, we were able to produce completely different emails, suitable for various types of content, without costing a penny of extra engineering, since the template recycled the code from the same original base template (FIG 3.4).

As you can see, there's a considerable range of flexibility, especially for a process that cuts back on engineering and requires zero design. That's right, we completely stopped designing product emails. For each email, I simply tell the engineers which template to use and which blocks to null within the template. No need for a mockup.

The only time I pull in a designer is if I want to use an icon or image block and need a new one we've never used before. The designers will create it and add it to the library (FIG 3.5),

Base template   Sample email

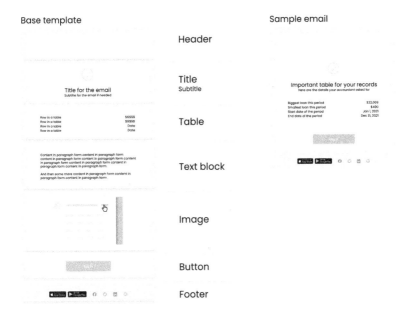

Header

Title
Subtitle

Table

Text block

Image

Button

Footer

FIG 3.3: Each template is made up of a finite set of content blocks that I could write or omit each time we create a new email.

FIG 3.4: A few templates can produce a large variety of email content structures, optimizing for both engineering and design investment, as well as user experience.

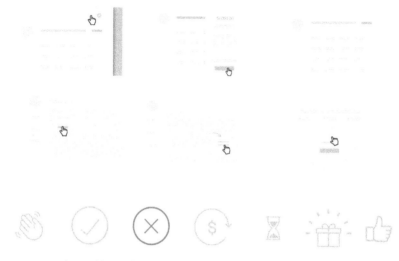

FIG 3.5: We have a library of icons and images that can be easily accessed and recycled in emails that include icon and image content blocks.

where engineers can find it at any time, without altering the original block.

Setting up this system did require an initial investment, but the long-term return was so obvious that getting business buy-in was easy. The concept of streamlining should be welcomed from everyone who proposes a way to do it.

But what about the existing emails? Aligning those was a little harder. I prioritized them by volume (are we sending a particular email twenty times a month or twenty thousand?) and impact (an email going to three hundred users, if optimized, can motivate them to complete an action that generates significant revenue for the business, while a different email going to a thousand users each month might be for regulatory purposes and not generate revenue at all). We were able to migrate a big chunk—but not all—of the emails already in the code. The rest we've updated slowly, sometimes in sprints where I've used UXW to save development time, and then laid claim to the surplus for the email project.

As a UXer, my initial motivation for this template project was to improve the experience, but the business benefits were also clear: namely, the engineering and design resources we saved. This made it very easy to talk about the ROI with business stakeholders. Finding that shared language and empathizing with each other's perspectives was (and continues to be) critical for our mutual success.

UXW doesn't improve ROI by magic. There are very clear mechanics for how it works. Once we have business stakeholders' buy-in and support, it's time to put UXW to work. Identifying these specific mechanisms of action can help us lean into them at the right moments and break down what we do for business stakeholders. After all, the more they understand the technical side of our job, the more they'll be able to appreciate and get behind investing in our work—and give informed feedback that makes it even better.

DECREASE FRICTION

Sometimes all we need to do is get out of the user's way. We don't need to help them along or push them forward; we just need to clear their path so that they can continue on their own.

There are many kinds of obstacles—friction—that can slow a user down. The friction of filling out a form can be reduced by prepopulating fields; the friction of opting into a service can be reduced by prechecking a box; the friction of understanding the next step in a flow can be reduced with better explanations. Each time we remove a barrier, lower a hurdle, or make getting from point *A* to point *B* easier, we decrease friction—which, with UXW, generally means a low investment and a high return.

Help users help themselves

Sarah Walsh and her team at Citibank rewrote a form and nearly doubled the amount of existing copy. Though concision is often preferable, if we don't give users what they need, we're not doing them any favors. Apparently, this form didn't have enough information and users were getting stuck.

Open	Confirm	Deposit

Complete the profile for other owners.

We ask for this information so we can protect you and us from things like fraud. It's part of compliance with the Currency and Foreign Transactions Reporting Act.

Kristina Durant

Ownership 27%

Residential Street Address   Apt/Unit (if applicable)

1893 Oakwood Avenue

Use the address found on your government documents. Sorry, no P.O. Box numbers.

City	State	ZIP Code
New York	NY	10013

Email Address

Buturing8149@example.com

We'll use this if we need to during application review.

Personal Phone Number

(212) 625-2652   Mobile

Enter a U.S based phone number

Social Security Number(SSN) or Taxpayer Identification Number(TIN)

XXX-XX-4567

Enter the owner's 9-digit national tax identification number

Date of Birth

05   26   1980

Before the rewrite, users would sometimes spend three to four minutes on a single field—and that's a lot of friction. Walsh's team used UXW to reduce the friction and, after adding helpful microcopy, users were spending three to four minutes on a *page*. Before the rewrite, 26 percent of users were completing the form; after the rewrite, that number went up to 92 percent. That's a huge jump in conversion without any additional outbound sales calls, or follow-up marketing emails to get users back into the flow they abandoned, or campaigns to draw users back from competitors they went to instead of finishing the Citibank flow. Reducing friction meant users got to where they were going anyway, but more quickly and with higher rates of success.

All of this is good for business, and I want to highlight not just what this copy *made* for the business, but what it *saved* for the business. UXW doesn't have to stop at increasing return; it can also decrease investment. In this case, the number of support calls dropped significantly (**FIG 3.6**). Citibank could now invest less in fielding calls and reallocate those resources for the improvement of other areas (https://bkaprt.com/buxw43/03-04, video).

Remove technical barriers

Decreasing friction isn't only about giving users more information so that they can get where they're going confidently and more quickly; it can also be about solving technical challenges. For example, if a user wants to give you their routing number but doesn't know where to find it, a little microcopy preempting that question and explaining where to look reduces friction by removing the technical barrier.

I once ran into this exact scenario. I was writing a touchpoint where users needed to enter their routing number but were not always sure where to find it. In this case, they didn't need to be sold on the competitive advantage of the product or anything like that; they just needed help figuring out how to do what they, and the business, wanted done. So, we wrote a tooltip to help them overcome the technical barrier (**FIG 3.7**).

Thanks to UXW, support and engineering resources that were being allocated to compensate for user errors at this critical step decreased significantly. I imagine relieving friction at this point led to increased completions of the flow as well. Not only can UXW decrease investment and increase return, but it can do both at the same time, smoothing out interactions so users can more efficiently get things done.

Joshua Porter, who coined the term "microcopy" in 2009, worked on a checkout flow where users were having similar issues with entering the correct billing address. By adding helper text next to the billing address input field ("Be sure to enter the billing address associated with your credit card"), he helped both users and the business get what they wanted (**FIG 3.8**) (https://bkaprt.com/buxw43/03-05).

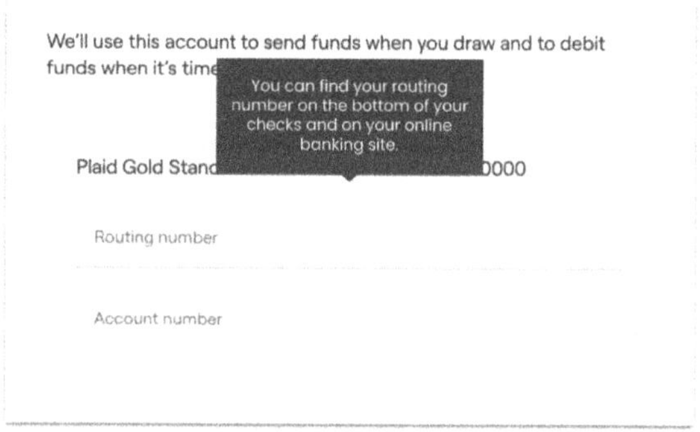

We'll use this account to send funds when you draw and to debit funds when it's time

You can find your routing number on the bottom of your checks and on your online banking site.

Plaid Gold Stand...0000

Routing number

Account number

FIG 3.7: Tooltip copy can help users overcome technical barriers.

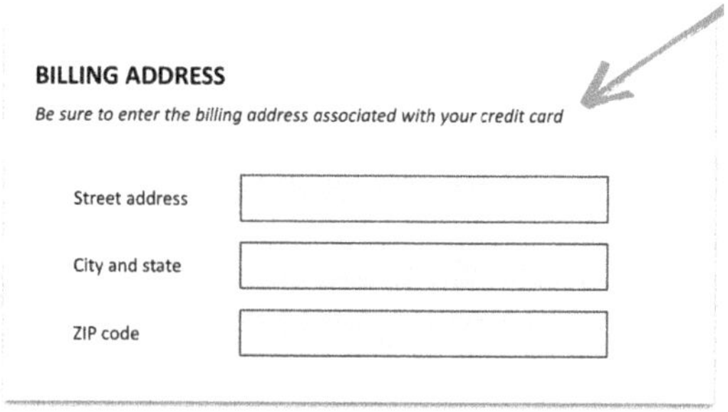

BILLING ADDRESS

Be sure to enter the billing address associated with your credit card

Street address

City and state

ZIP code

FIG 3.8: This mockup of a billing address form includes a sentence that preempts a common point of friction in a purchase flow, helping more users spend money faster.

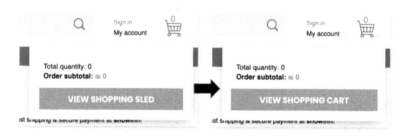

FIG 3.9: This mockup of an ecommerce site's purchasing flow shows how a minimal investment—changing one word on a button—can make a big difference for users.

On an ecommerce site that specializes in winter sports gear, the element we all traditionally know as a shopping cart was called a shopping *sled* (**FIG 3.9**). The company was trying to be unique and express its brand voice, but there is a time to stand out and a time to align with existing conventions. Users were expecting to find things they wanted to pay for in a cart, not a sled. When interviewed, 50 percent of users said that they could not find their cart at all while the other 50 percent said that they found it by relying on other UX conventions like the location and behavior of the icon (https://bkaprt.com/buxw43/03-06). I can guarantee you that when users can find the things they want to pay for, it's good for the business's bottom line. Beware of creating technical barriers where there weren't any to begin with!

It takes research and empathy to predict technical barriers. We need to understand not only where users are getting stuck, but why. Once we uncover a point of friction that UXW can reduce, we have a great opportunity for increasing ROI with our work.

DRIVE MOTIVATION

Sometimes we need to reduce friction, removing barriers for users so they can get where they were going anyway. Other times we need to encourage users, cheering from behind instead of pulling down roadblocks in front. The first step is to find out what motivates them. What's going through their heads when they're deciding whether to continue, and what information should we reinforce or dispel to urge them forward?

Confidence

As we saw in the Google hotels example (**FIG 1.2**), empathizing with users can make a world of difference in terms of ROI. We do this by meeting users where they are, understanding what's holding them back, and surfacing the things that make them feel confident enough to move forward.

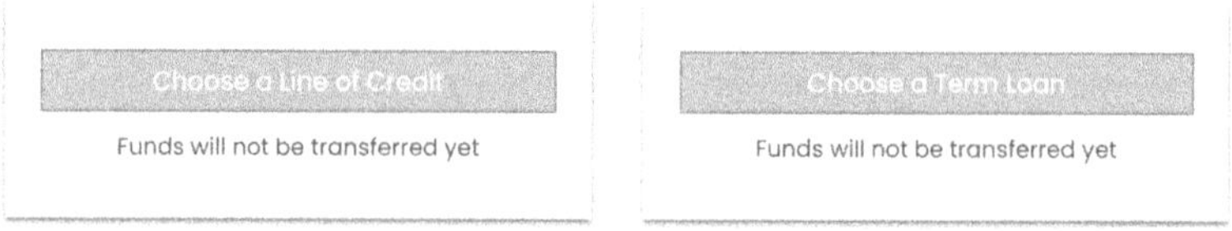

Choose a Line of Credit	Choose a Term Loan
Funds will not be transferred yet	Funds will not be transferred yet

FIG 3.10: Empathetic helper text addresses users' hesitations, helping them get through the flow.

In a flow I worked on, users who applied for credit could be approved for two types of financing: a credit line and a term loan. They first needed to select the type of financing they wanted, and then later make more detailed decisions like how much to borrow and how to repay.

We discovered that users were dropping off after being *approved* for credit! They'd made it past the entire application, and yet they weren't accepting the financing they'd been approved for. Why? It turns out that many were hesitant because they thought that the moment they committed to an offer, the maximum amount of funds they were approved for would immediately be transferred to their account—even if they wanted to borrow less—without a chance to even review, let alone choose, repayment terms. To fix this problem, we met the users where they were and wrote helper text below the CTA, assuring them that no funds would be transferred yet (**FIG 3.10**).

One of our main inspirations for using helper text in this way was an Amazon purchase flow that did the same thing for similar reasons (**FIG 3.11**). The use case here is a user reaching the end of a purchase flow and realizing at the last second that they want to update their payment method. They jump to the screen where they can do that, and then they're ready to get back to their purchase. To do that, they need to click "Continue" and Amazon's helper text reassures them that this is just to get back to where they were, not to complete the purchase on the spot. Remember, the user was in the middle of reviewing order details when they realized they needed to update their payment method. They still may have wanted to make decisions about shipping method and gift wrap. They could have been afraid to

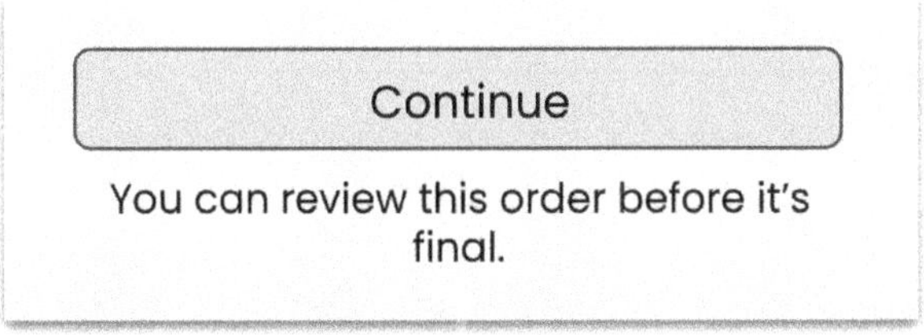

> **Continue**
>
> You can review this order before it's final.

FIG 3.11: Empathetic helper text in the Amazon app addresses users' hesitations and helps them get through the flow.

click "Continue" from the payment method page if they thought doing that might complete the purchase then and there.

In both cases, the helper text does not distract from the CTA, while appearing exactly when the user is deciding how motivated they are to click or tap it. They want to keep going but need a critical answer to a question before feeling confident enough to move forward. A little string—a small investment—is all it sometimes takes to help users make the purchase, take the loan offer, or do whatever else increases return for the business.

Incentive and opportunity

Users come to the product to achieve something, and sometimes all it takes to motivate them to keep going is a reminder about what awaits them at the end of the flow. Combining a reminder to take action with an opportunity to take that same action—or a path toward taking it—is another way low-investment copy can produce big returns.

I once worked on a product where our value to users depended on insight into the users' accounting software. If the user did not connect their software, we served an empty state, because without that connection, we had nothing to show (FIG 3.12). We could've left the empty state informative: "There are no invoices to see here because you have not connected your accounting software." End of story. Instead, we took the opportunity to motivate action. We left no room for users to wonder what their next steps were or why they should take them. We

Your available credit
$3,200 of $5,000

Upcoming payment
$11,527
Nov 25, 2015

Connect accounting software

Once you connect your accounting software, your invoices will appear
here and you'll be able to draw advances from your credit line.

FIG 3.12: Empty states are a great place to provide incentives and opportunities that motivate action.

even included a CTA so they could immediately do what we'd just explained they needed to do in order to use the product. If the copy didn't motivate action, these users might not have restored their dashboard to a state in which they could get cash advances—which is not good for them or for the business.

The American Red Cross uses microcopy to motivate users who are near the end of a donation flow. Many donors want to be able to choose a specific cause. However, other donors who don't care about choosing a cause still want to know which cause they're donating to and want to be confident their donation is going to something important even if they don't actively choose anything. These potential donors may drop off because they can't or don't want to decide where to donate and the dropdown requires them to.

The Red Cross aims to keep a good number of these donors in the game through microcopy in the dropdown (FIG 3.13). This microcopy assures users that their donation will indeed do good, even if they prefer not to take on the cognitive load of choosing a specific cause. There was no technical barrier or lack of communication between the product and the user in this case; there was simply a missed opportunity for enthusiasm.

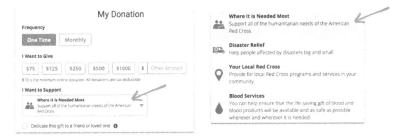

FIG 3.13: Helper text can motivate action.

Imbuing confidence and articulating incentive or next steps are two examples of how microcopy can motivate users to complete flows with low investment and high return. Sometimes, users need us to reduce friction and remove obstacles. Other times, there are no real obstacles, but there are distractions and fatigue, and users need a little push to keep them going. Once we provide that, they get closer to achieving their goals and we improve ROI for our organization, all at once.

ENHANCE REPUTATION

UXW also increases ROI by enhancing the reputation of the product and the brand. It may be harder to measure the return of an enhanced reputation than it is to lower friction or increase motivation in product flows, but it's just as important. To enhance reputation, we can write copy that is more ethical by being more accessible and inclusive. We can also write copy that is delightful and professional, increasing perceived brand integrity.

All other things being equal, the return will be higher for an organization with such a reputation. That said, we can't really quantify how much people trust a brand or tell their friends that a product is of high quality. We can try to use *Net Promoter Scores* (NPS) and analyze mentions on social media to survey churned users, or something similar. But no quantitative measure will fully capture the qualitative impact of product reputation and brand perception.

Brand perception

Starbucks has a delightful user experience where, instead of calling out your coffee order when it's ready ("tall double-skinny latte, extra hot!"), they'll call your name. It's a nice personal touch and personalization is known to improve quantitative metrics in email open rates and conversion. But there's an edge case: the barista has no idea how to write a certain user's name, comparable to when the backend fails to accurately pull a parameter from the database and ends up serving an email that starts with, "Hi none." In the digital case, as a UX writer, I always recommend coding a fallback—basically an if-then statement that tells the front end: "If no variable found, serve 'Hi there.'"

What fallback works at Starbucks? One creative barista wrote the message, "I am STILL going to spell your name horribly, horribly wrong." In a moment of potential friction—or in the case of a neutral fallback, a missed opportunity—the barista created a moment of delight. Can I quantitatively prove that this experience has increased the *lifetime value* (LTV) of this user to the business? Of course not. But the photo of this interaction appeared on Instagram, framing Starbucks in a positive light. People feel good about the brand's empathy and the product's delight. That can only increase users' willingness to spend money (which is good for the business), and their enjoyment of the product (which is good for the user). Once again, it's UXW for the win-win.

Accessibility

Tech is the future. It's unethical to limit innovations in tech to a select few. If tech evolves only for certain groups, privilege is exacerbated and the chasm between the haves and the have-nots deepens, depriving us all of synergy left untapped. Products are more useful, businesses more successful, and humanity better off when tech behaves ethically—and UXW has a big role to play in that.

Accessibility means making products usable for people who might otherwise face barriers to entry beyond their control.

Originally, permanent physical barriers were at the core of the conversation, and screen readers used by people with visual impairments were the primary use case. "Accessibility" at that time was often a buzzword for alt text and similar UXW tools and techniques used for making visual UI accessible to people who consume content in ways that are not dependent on sight.

Over time, the accessibility conversation broadened to include not only additional permanent physical barriers like color vision deficiency, but also long-term, nonphysical barriers like neurodiversity, low literacy, and low digital literacy; temporary barriers like injury; and situational barriers like a new parent dealing with constant distractions and extreme fatigue, or a person trying to use a voice interface in a loud, public space.

It's easy to see how making products accessible to those with permanent, temporary, and situational barriers to entry is ethical, but it also makes good (business) sense. Without accommodating people who experience these barriers, a huge potential market—an estimated 18 percent of the population in the UK lives with a disability (https://bkaprt.com/buxw43/03-07)—is off-limits to the business. Furthermore, accessibility is becoming a legal requirement in more countries, and risking lawsuits is not in the business's best interest (Web Content Accessibility Guidelines [WCAG] 2.1) (https://bkaprt.com/buxw43/03-08).

Writing alt text for images and meaningful link text (as opposed to "Learn more" and "Click here") makes visual content accessible to users who, for any number of reasons, consume content using screen readers. Closed captioning on videos helps lower barriers to consuming audio content for those who are hard of hearing or located in a quiet library or on loud public transportation. Alt text, meaningful link text, and closed captioning all fall within the realm of UXW (https://bkaprt.com/buxw43/03-09).

We can write without reference to design elements like "tabs" and "windows," or to tech jargon like "navigate," to make flows accessible to people with low digital literacy. We can use tools like Hemingway App (https://bkaprt.com/buxw43/03-10) to make sure we keep our copy at an accessible reading level for everyone, and we can apply evidence-based recommendations

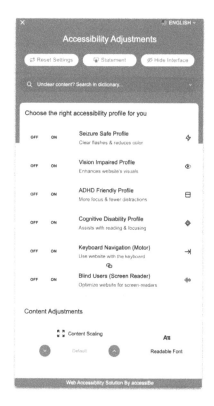

FIG 3.14: A third-party widget by accessiBe provides an out-of-the-box accessibility solution for websites and digital products (https://bkaprt.com/buxw43/03-12).

FIG 3.15: Instagram uses inclusive copy in notifications.

in the crowd-sourced Readability Guidelines (https://bkaprt.com/buxw43/03-11). These are all in the UX writer's purview.

Products can also integrate out-of-the-box solutions, including accessiBe (**FIG 3.14**), which can help us catch the lowest-hanging fruit until we're able to expand our in-house accessibility efforts.

There's an ocean of resources out there for making products more accessible, which you can find in the Resources section. Diving into them all is not within the scope of this book, but any book about using UXW to improve the business and user experience would not be complete without touching on accessibility.

Inclusivity

Like accessibility, making products inclusive is not just ethical—it also increases a business's success by appealing to more people. While it's obvious that using language that resonates with and includes more people will increase the number of users, the quality of users, the stickiness of the product, and the virality of the product, the overall impact of inclusivity is not tied directly to any quantitative metric. It's not really tangible.

Inclusivity—also known as *diversity, equity, and inclusion* (DEI)—needs to be addressed not only within businesses' internal structures and cultures, but also in the UI that businesses serve to their users. The ROI of DEI could be a whole book unto itself. We'll just touch on the surface here.

The absolute basics of inclusive UXW means using language that applies equally to all genders, races, religions, and sexual orientations. This is one reason why the singular they/their/them has become so popular lately. It's now considered both correct and a best practice to write, "Once the *user* completes *their* purchase, we'll send a receipt."

Instagram uses the singular "they" when notifying me that my friend Shir (she/her) mentioned me in her story (FIG 3.15). The Instagram copy says that Shir mentioned me in "their" story, because Instagram doesn't know how Shir identifies—and doesn't need to. Using "their" means Instagram gets it right for every user no matter how they identify.

Gender inclusivity is not the only type of inclusivity we need to consider when writing product copy. For example, there are often validation errors on input fields that are ethnically, culturally, or otherwise exclusive—like requiring a last name to be at least three characters when many common Chinese names are two (FIG 3.16). Perhaps this validation was put in place as an anti-spam measure or to prevent user error, but that doesn't excuse its exclusive nature; a different mechanism could have replaced it. If inclusivity were top of mind, the copy might

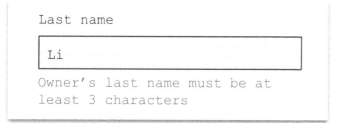

FIG 3.16: Non-inclusive microcopy still abounds.

instead prompt the user to confirm the input, rather than prevent them from continuing until they make a "correction."

These kinds of bad user experiences happen not only when names are given a minimum or maximum character count, but also when special characters such as hyphens or umlauts are excluded. Even if, due to a technical limitation, not all users will be able to input their names correctly, good copy can still solve the friction by expressing empathy, providing information about the limitation, and otherwise showing awareness and sensitivity.

LOCALIZATION

The use of special characters in name fields is an inclusivity issue, but it also highlights localization considerations. First, localization is not the same as translation. Translation means translating the words; localization means translating the experience. Localization needs to be layered on top of translation so that when products expand to new markets, they translate their experiences to match the local culture, norms, and sensitivities.

When we translate a product without localizing the experience as a whole, we serve the original language's cultural lens, references, common understanding, and biases to the new user base. Not only will a lot of the product not make sense in the new language if directly translated, but—despite using the new language's words and grammatical structure—it's likely to step on some toes or even cause serious offense. It might be better to avoid those markets altogether than to translate them without localization.

Regardless of the product's availability in multiple languages, we should stay away from idioms, metaphors, puns, and the like to remove barriers for low-literacy or transregional folks. Translation makes this best practice even more important. Even if we're not translating idioms word for word, instead using the nearest native idiom in the new language, we still risk dragging in all kinds of associations and nuances—some potentially harmful, and all unintentional.

Expanding into new markets is by and large good. It's better for users when more people in the world get to enjoy the product, and it's obviously better for businesses when more people do what the product has set out to have them do. To gain wide appeal, we typically adjust our voice to resonate with our audience. But when our audience is spread across many cultures, we need to localize that voice to scale.

GETTING IT DONE

If there's one message I hope you take away from this book, it's that good UXW is as much a science as it is an art. It's not the creative writing of poets and novelists; it's a tool that, if used correctly, businesses should use to impact their ultimate success and improve users' experience.

Many of us explain what UXW is and argue that it matters, but once we've caught the ear of those who need to hear us, the next level of resolution is to explain exactly how UXW does what it does. By decreasing friction and increasing motivation for users, enhancing our products' reputations, and putting more ethically positive experiences into the world, we unleash the true power of UXW. But it's only through the measurement of our work's success that we can communicate this power with concrete, tangible evidence on our side.

SHOW ME THE MONEY: MEASURING SUCCESS

I STARTED EXPLORING HOW to prove the impact of UXW with cold hard numbers because I noticed there was a void. Conferences, blogs, and podcasts untangled fascinating and evolving subjects like accessibility, inclusivity, localization, personalization, content design, product content strategy, conversation design, heuristics, organizational structures, career paths, and even what to call ourselves—but there was almost nothing about proving our efficacy. Diving into this vertical was a way for me to make a unique contribution to the global community.

I certainly haven't discovered it all—and since heading down this particular rabbit hole, I've found that I'm not the only one down here—but I can start shining the spotlight on an additional area of our field that deserves attention and investment.

Data-driven UXW came naturally to me. Before pivoting into UXW, I spent ten years in neurobiology, where every narrative, every discovery, was inseparable from the data. The truth and value of anything we did was inherently intertwined with *quantitative data* specifically, and yet, on its own, it was insufficient. Context and interpretation were equally vital to understanding our findings. That appreciation for quantitative and qualitative measurements of success translates fluidly to the world of UXW.

BEFORE YOU MEASURE A THING

As Torrey Podmajersky explained in *Strategic Writing for UX*, if we don't measure what we're doing, we can't improve it. It's critical to measure the impact of our work; but for those measurements to be meaningful, we first need to set the foundation. We need to choose the right metrics to measure, ensure we use multiple metrics for more holistic insights, set benchmarks before we measure so we can make a comparison afterwards, and prepare ourselves for where it might all go wrong. Let's dig a little deeper into these foundational elements.

Choose the right metrics

What should we measure? Well, that depends on the business goal we're aiming for. It's critical to choose metrics that will serve as accurate proxies for what we want to know. For example, if we're wondering whether a specific email increases conversion in the product, the open rate of the email isn't an appropriate metric. We'd need to measure the user's behavior *after* they open the email, not measure *whether* they open the email.

That example may sound straightforward, but it can be surprising to learn how often we measure what's easiest, using whatever analytics already exist within the business—even if they're not the most indicative of the answer we're looking for. As I mentioned in Chapter 3, we definitely want to leverage those "freebies." But we also need to think critically about which ones are relevant and, if necessary, build the infrastructure to collect the data that can fully answer our specific questions.

Set benchmarks

Benchmarking means choosing a quantitative metric, such as time on task, conversion, number of returning visitors, or any other numerical representation of some aspect of the experience (https://bkaprt.com/buxw43/04-01). It's a basic springboard for measuring improvement. Choosing and finding that baseline is a fundamental first step in proving and communicating ROI. Benchmarking serves the same purpose as control groups in experiments. Both are critical because our success or failure is always relative.

Use multiple metrics

In an episode of the *NN/g UX Podcast,* Kate Moran warned us that data should inform design, not lead it (https://bkaprt.com/ buxw43/04-02). It's important not to let quantitative data make design decisions for us. Avoid putting too much emphasis on a single metric; instead, measure as many different angles as possible to produce the most meaningful insights. We need to remember that *what gets measured is what gets managed.* So, if we focus on measuring one thing, we'll pour all of our efforts into managing and optimizing that thing, and we'll start making decisions solely based on whether that one number is going up or down.

Think back to our earlier example of the Draw Funds flow. If we measure only the frequency of draws and not the dollar amounts of each draw, or calls to customer support asking to reverse the draw because the flow was so frictionless that the draw was made by mistake, we'll then focus all of our tests on continuing to increase frequency, when at the end of the day, that was not the ultimate business goal—optimal drawing was. However, if we measure from multiple angles, we can combine the data to determine whether we've actually succeeded.

An example of what *not* to do comes from the use of "manipu-links" or "confirm-shaming." This is when secondary CTAs require the user to say something negative about themselves like, "No, I don't like saving money," or, "I don't want to stay up to date" (FIG 4.1).

When we focus on only one metric—in this case, the click-through rate—writing unethical copy becomes scarily easy. We think it's sufficient because we don't bother to consider other factors; our compensation or even our job security depends on quick problem-solving. But think past that initial number for a second: Does tricking people into signing up for newsletters increase revenue or anything else of value for the business?

FIG 4.1: Confirm-shaming, unfortunately, is still abundant. It's a problematic pattern that doesn't work in the short or long run. Even if you shame a user into subscribing to a newsletter, the chances of that turning into a sale—after ruining the emotional relationship—is low (https://bkaprt.com/buxw43/04-02).

We can all agree it's terrible for the user. Signups may increase, sure, but is anyone going to read a newsletter they didn't mean to sign up for? Are they even going to open the email, let alone convert later in the funnel?

This is an example of how a single data point can support a bad copy decision, whereas multiple data points from across the user journey might've balanced our priorities to serve users better. At the end of the day, we might decide that less aggressive (and more ethical) copy, even with decreasing signups, increases the LTV of the users who do sign up—because their intent matches the flow endpoints better.

If we want to know whether a certain subject line increases open rates, we're going to measure open rates, but we might also want to measure unsubscribes, because if more people are opening the email only to unsubscribe from the mailing list, we're probably not achieving our goal. And that goal isn't really to increase open rates, is it? It's to increase the number of users reading the body of the email, consuming the messaging, and hopefully acting on it. If we gain eyes on this email but pay for it through users unsubscribing, overall engagement has not improved.

Similarly, in the example from Chapter 1 (where the business goal was to decrease drop-off in a credit application flow) we would need to measure the difference in drop-off between users in a control group and in a test group, as well as the LTV of the users we "saved" with our test copy. Or maybe LTV isn't the best metric—and certainly not the only one—we could use as a proxy for the quality of users we saved. Maybe we'd need a more immediate indication, like utilization during the first week or the amount of the first draw. That resolution is beyond the scope of this book. But the takeaway is the same as in the example about open rates—experiments are not one-dimensional. It's not enough to simply measure drop-off here, because our goal isn't really to decrease drop-off—it's to increase revenue for the business. If we decrease the drop-off of unprofitable users, we haven't reached our real goal.

Throughout all of this, we must maintain a holistic view of the experience and user journey—and, in turn, their impact on the business's growth. This approach fuels design decisions that are in everyone's best interest, because we're designing to improve the whole product, instead of, for example, letting one number determine whether we need to change a string. We're more in control of the design when we step back and look at the big picture.

Beware of bias

There may be no greater opportunity to fall into a bias trap than when measuring the success or failure of a copy solution. Naturally, we want our solution to work, so much so that we're likely to push extra hard for success in the data instead of staying neutral. But it's okay if the first or second or third solution doesn't work—we just move to the next one on the list, which will be better informed than the last. A few examples of bias at this stage include:

- **Recruitment.** A simple example of bias in data collection is how we recruit participants. Are we only posting in certain

Facebook groups where we're likely to get participants who are similar to us and one another? On usertesting.com, I often end up with 100 percent of my participants being the same gender as I am. I'll usually run the test again—and if I don't, I'll at least integrate that awareness into my interpretations of the data later.

- **Being blinded by our personal perspective.** We're human. It's normal to have an interest in a certain version of the copy winning out, but we should never let that affect our interpretation of the data. Mitigating bias in qualitative research is particularly challenging because it means putting our ego on the shelf. We all come from unique backgrounds that create gaps in our view of the world, so reliable data is dependent on us proactively acknowledging and correcting for our biases.
- **Paying more attention to the loudest users.** The loudest users are often the most unhappy, not the most representative. That doesn't mean our data isn't valuable! This "loud" feedback can in fact be a blessing in disguise, highlighting the lowest-hanging fruit for us to address. Remember: small improvements can still have a big impact. We can't get down on ourselves when we see a disproportionate number of negative comments, because they're not necessarily representative of the user base at large.
- **Considering unwanted variables.** Bias goes beyond our desired outcomes and skewed interpretations. Data collection and interpretation can also be affected by confounding factors outside of our control, some of which we may never have been able to expect. After all, we're not running tests in a sterile lab; we're running them in the real world. What if there's an economic crisis during the test period? How could that affect user behavior? We can hope that it affects the test and control groups similarly, and so there is still validity to the outcomes, but that may not always be the case.

Say we're testing the hypothesis that our brand is perceived as not being in touch with current events, which is hurting conversion. We create a copy test where the control group sees the unchanged UI, which does not address current events, and the test group sees a version of the copy that discusses an upcoming local election. We're in the middle of running the test when, suddenly, there's a local political scandal. We could never have predicted this would happen or planned our test around it. In this case, the scandal only affects the test group, who may interact with the product differently because of how they feel about the scandal, not because of how "with it" the copy feels. If the test group's "current events copy" were about a hurricane and not a political scandal, it wouldn't have affected the groups differently, and we would be able to isolate the effects of the "current events copy" without the influence of users' reactions to a specific, triggering current event.

If confounding factors affect the test and control groups in various ways, the results may be more complicated to interpret and less credible overall. There's not necessarily a good way to mitigate this, but having awareness is important for analyzing the data in a meaningful and nuanced way.

Paying the price

Metrics let us know whether our copy succeeded...or failed, which is always an option. Once business stakeholders recognize the potential impact of UXW, they'll want to work with us to increase ROI; however, their new understanding also means they have insight into the potential negative impact of getting UXW wrong. Like fire, UXW can be used for good or evil—for shining a light in the darkness or burning the whole place down. As excited as business stakeholders may be to empower UX writers to do more, they may also have new hesitations.

For example, say you want to run a test comparing existing copy (the control) to supposedly improved copy (the test). While it's true that the test variant may improve metrics, it may also do the opposite. We don't know—which is the whole point of the test. Business stakeholders may invest in copy tests because they understand the potential impact of small UXW changes on ROI, but they might also have the valid concern that, if a specific test variant has a negative impact, the outcome might be worse than never having run the test at all.

In *Presenting Design Work*, Donna Spencer reminded us that part of communicating and empathizing with business stakeholders is remembering that they have a vested interest in our work—for better or worse.

> *There is usually someone in a business who owns the overall product. This person also usually owns the risk. They're financially responsible and also responsible for what happens when the product or service goes out into the world. Although designers sometimes think they make the design decisions, ultimately, it's this person who makes final decisions about the design—it's their risk they're managing.*

Business stakeholders are on the front lines of the company; they have their own higher-ups to report to and performance metrics to meet. As mentioned earlier, KPIs are often tied to revenue metrics (such as profit and cost savings) and to how people are evaluated (bonuses they receive or budgets they're given to expand their teams). Speaking the same language as these stakeholders means empathizing with their role, concerns, and personal risk in our UXW projects.

The good news is that there's an easy approach to empathizing with their point of view:

1. Recognize their concern.
2. Ask questions to understand the specifics of their risk.
3. Implement fail-safes to mitigate risk and communicate those clearly to the business stakeholder. There are plenty of ways to mitigate risk, such as running tests on a small percentage of users (e.g., 5 percent in the control group and 5 percent in the test group and—once everyone's comfortable that no damage is being done—opening the test to 50 percent in each group).

Not only is this important for collaboration going forward, but it's also important for the business now. Operating under the assumption that the stakeholders' hesitations are founded in the business's best interests, you'll find that addressing them sets up healthy practices on both a personal level and a business level.

QUANTITATIVE METRICS

There are lots of tools and methods out there for capturing success or failure. It can be tempting to grab the cheapest or most easily available, but we can't succumb to that temptation. We must wisely choose the tools and methods that will provide the most value for a given project.

A/B testing

A/B testing is one of the most common quantitative testing methods. It's pretty straightforward: we put one version of the copy in front of one audience, and (keeping everything else equal) another version of the copy in front of a comparable audience. Then, we measure whatever we're measuring—like the number of users who click on the button with the control copy versus test copy—and see which group gets a higher score. An article on BBC's Global Experience Language website lists button clicks, time on task, task completion rate, task drop-off rate, error occurrence rate, and conversion as other possible metrics for this type of test (https://bkaprt.com/buxw43/04-03).

Pros and cons of A/B testing:

- **Pros:** We get solid numbers, which can give us a feeling of confidence in the results and lend strong support to whatever hypothesis they align with. Fifty clicks versus five hundred is easy for anyone to understand and hard to argue with.
- **Cons:** A/B testing can only tell us what happened—not why. This is a critical drawback, and one that can be compensated for in a mixed-methods approach by supplementing data with appropriate qualitative findings. Consider a scenario where the goal is to get more people to click on a button to transfer funds into their account. The control says "Transfer Funds" and the test variant says "Continue," and once it's all

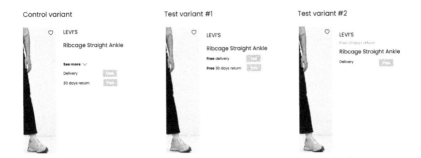

Control variant   Test variant #1   Test variant #2

FIG 4.2: This example A/B/C test, similar to what Zalora would have used, includes a control and two variants to test microcopy.

said and done, the test variant gets ten times as many clicks. We now know *what* happened (the test version worked better) but not *why*. In this case, we would need to talk to users—what if they were more likely to click on "Continue" because they expected to get more information about their repayment terms but didn't? If they were clicking more times but for the wrong reasons, that's not a win. Do not trust A/B test results in a vacuum.

ZALORA, an online retailer, had the goal of increasing the number of checkouts by highlighting two popular features: free returns and free delivery. The team hypothesized that users were not aware of the features because of their poor visibility on the website: the features were hidden under "See more" on the original page (https://bkaprt.com/buxw43/04-04). So the team created a test variant that not only pulled the copy out from behind a click, but also promoted the copy in the content hierarchy on the page. The second test variant also surfaced this copy from behind the click, but front-loaded the word "Free," too (**FIG 4.2**).

Test variant #1 won, improving checkouts by 12.3 percent. That's of course before the team validated the *why* with qualitative methods—and cleaning the data for bias and any other confounding factors. However, the raw data looked promising.

Note that a test variant won't always win. There will be times when what we had to begin with was better than the alternatives we tested it against, and that's okay. First of all, we can pat ourselves on the back for having done well in the past. Next, we can come up with a new set of variations to test; optimization never ends. Alternatively, we can choose to end the testing—concluding that, on this touchpoint, we have reached a point of diminishing returns—and move on to a different business goal.

Single Ease Question (SEQ)

The SEQ is a one-question survey administered immediately after a task. It uses a (usually) seven-point rating scale to assess the difficulty of a task for users and is often built into the product, appearing on screen during the flow (**FIG 4.3**).

It may be helpful to use an SEQ together with an A/B test, comparing the results of each. If the test variant was clicked more (A/B) and also ranked as easier (SEQ), great! But what if it was clicked less and also ranked as easier? That might indicate that we should look somewhere earlier in the flow for a more effective optimization.

An SEQ is different from a *net promoter score* (NPS), although they may look and feel similar. NPS data is more relevant for product marketing research, whereas SEQ tells us more about usability.

Pros and cons of SEQ:

- **Pros:** SEQ is relatively reliable and very efficient. Because it's so frictionless for the user, you're likely to get high participation rates, and because it's easy to analyze, you can get robust data quickly. It also shows how users feel, which A/B testing can't reveal on its own.
- **Cons:** Users may not accurately report the difficulty of a given task. If they "failed" or took longer than expected, there's a chance they won't admit it to protect their ego; we're all human, after all. Users also tend to rate more time-consuming tasks as more difficult, even if they were easy. For example, filling in your name and address is easy, but if the task is broken up into separate fields—for first,

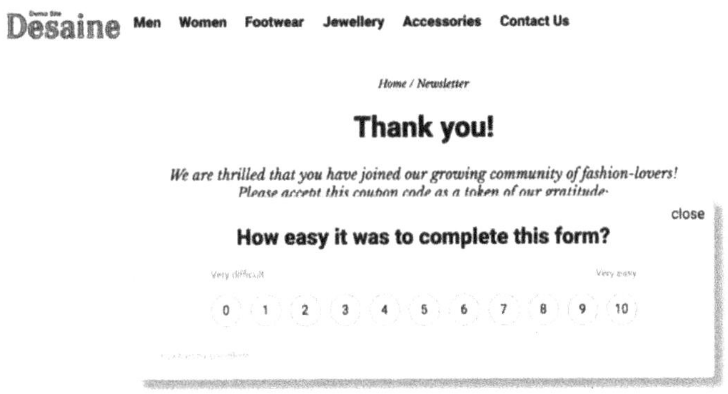

Desaine Men Women Footwear Jewellery Accessories Contact Us

Home / Newsletter

Thank you!

We are thrilled that you have joined our growing community of fashion-lovers!
Please accept this coupon code as a token of our gratitude.

close

How easy it was to complete this form?

Very difficult   Very easy

0   1   2   3   4   5   6   7   8   9   10

FIG 4.3: An in-product SEQ test can be a useful quantitative research tool.

middle, and last name, street, street number, apartment or suite number, city, state, ZIP, and country—it could take longer than expected, resulting in a disproportionately low SEQ score. If names appear as one field, street address as another, city/state as another, and ZIP as the last, we might get a better score, not accurately reflecting the level of usability we're testing for. We can try to normalize SEQ data for duration by crossing the data with a time-to-completion metric—a quantitative metric that's not dependent on subjective user input (https://bkaprt.com/buxw43/04-05).

When possible, combine a quantitative SEQ with a qualitative (free-text) survey to produce even more comprehensive insights (FIG 4.4).

Click tests

Click tests give users a task, recording where on the prototype they click to complete it. They can be used on one page or across an entire user journey. Clicks are usually analyzed by quantifying the location of first clicks or evaluating a heatmap, where colors indicate high to low volumes of clicks (https://bkaprt.com/buxw43/04-06).

FIG 4.4: In-product, free-text qualitative survey questions can be analyzed together with SEQ results.

Bob Bailey, a UX designer and researcher, ran a click test on the Centers for Disease Control and Prevention website in 2006. He found that a participant who clicks down the correct path on the first try will complete their task successfully 87 percent of the time, while a participant who clicks down the wrong path on the first try tends to successfully complete their task only 46 percent of the time (https://bkaprt.com/buxw43/04-07).

When trying to improve ROI, we want to increase revenue, which means we need users to complete the revenue-generating task at hand. If Bailey is right—and there's a 41 percent difference in the likelihood a user will complete their task based on their very first click—we'd better get the first click right! Focusing investment heavily on that first click, as opposed to evenly spreading our efforts throughout the flow, could pay off big time (https://bkaprt.com/buxw43/04-08).

Pros and cons of click tests:

- **Pros:** This type of testing produces clear, direct answers to usability questions such as, "Where would you click to complete your purchase?" Testing can be conducted on a static mockup, early-stage wireframe, final live public website, or anything in between. Click testing is also very low cost, unlike A/B testing, which requires engineering resources.

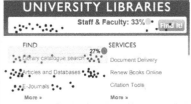

FIG 4.5: Raw results of a first-click study conducted at a Canadian university led to important insights about content hierarchy and undergraduate student users (https://bkaprt.com/buxw43/04-09).

- **Cons:** Click testing does not give us any insight into why users clicked what they clicked—unless combined with open-ended questions that were answered in person, out loud and recorded, or typed in as free text.

At a Canadian university, two hundred participants were asked to find journal articles, which is the top task for undergraduates and faculty at most university libraries. The university measured where participants first clicked on the website when trying to achieve that task (**FIG 4.5**). They found that undergraduates were more likely to use the search field. Undergraduates who tried to use category links instead often went to the wrong one. From these results, we can conclude that getting undergraduates to use the search field more and the category links less will translate into more effective, quicker searches, as well as less frustrating, more delightful, and more productive experiences.

Now imagine this is an ecommerce site, and instead of comparing undergraduates to faculty, we're comparing high-value shoppers to low-value shoppers. We find out that high-value shoppers are far more likely to look for products through the search field, and less likely to click on the wrong meta category listing for the products they're trying to buy. That's important information that we can collect quickly and credibly, information that can inform how we continue to design our navigation, search components, and browsing-to-purchase flows to increase revenue. The test itself has a very low cost, which of course, is good for ROI.

Card sorting

Card sorting is a method used for testing research menus and other navigational copy. Users are provided with cards—containing all kinds of feature names, product names, categories, and other elements that might help us build our information architecture—and asked to arrange them in sets.

Pros and cons of card sorting:

- **Pros:** This test is almost completely devoid of tester bias. While we do decide what is written on the cards, there are no leading questions and no specific variants we are hoping will win. Participants' insights here can open our minds to solutions we wouldn't have even thought to test with users or try in the product.
- **Cons:** To minimize bias, participants will be sorting the cards in a vacuum, with no context for the rest of the product or even the rest of the screen, which may impact the applicability of their decisions. They may also misunderstand the intention of the microcopy on certain cards, sorting them according to concepts that they don't represent.

Card sorting is particularly valuable for working on a navigation menu, for example (**FIG 4.6**). Let's say our research question is: Where would a new product name go that is *not* a credit product? Would we replace "Credit" with "Product?" In which case, what would we do with users who have access to only one of the products, or users who have access to a long list of products that would make the menu navigation more trouble than it's worth? We really don't know, so let's ask users.

We'll give them a deck of cards—with all kinds of categories, types of information, products, features, value props, and blank cards so that they can invent menu labels we hadn't thought of—and ask them to rearrange the menu in the way that would help them navigate the app as efficiently as possible (**FIG 4.7**). What makes sense to them intuitively may not be what makes

Before

After

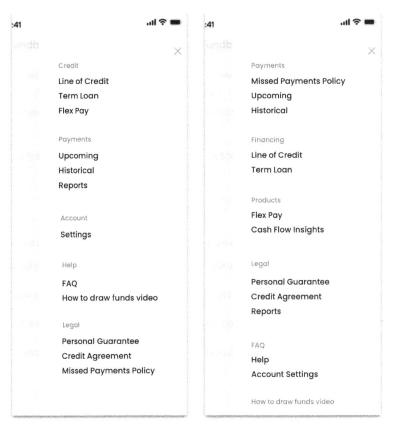

FIG 4.6: Here's a hamburger menu—before (left) and after (right) a card sort test—that needed reorganizing as the app evolved and the product offering grew.

sense to us, as we're blinded by the curse of already knowing about each menu item—but what matters is that it makes sense to them.

Test question

Credit	Payments	Account	Help	Legal	*Main labels*
Line of Credit	Upcoming	Settings	FAQ	Personal Guarantee	*Sub-labels*
Term Loan	Historical		How to draw funds video	Credit Agreement	
Flex Pay	Reports			Missed Payments Policy	

Cash Flow Insights   *Test question: Where does this card go?*

Unsorted cards

Historical, Account, Line of Credit, Upcoming, Settings, Reports, Missed Payments Policy, Cash Flow Insights, Help, Legal, How to draw funds video, Credit, Payments, Personal Guarantee, Credit Agreement, FAQ, Term Loan, Flex Pay

Test results

How to draw funds video	Legal	*Products*	*Financing*	FAQ	Payments	*Main labels*
	Personal Guarantee	Flex Pay	Line of Credit	Help	Missed Payments Policy	*Sub-labels*
	Credit Agreement	Cash Flow Insights	Term Loan	*Account Settings*	Upcoming	
	Reports				Historical	

Settings   Account   Credit   *Don't use*

FIG 4.7: A card sort for a menu would start with the UX writer's hypothesis of how the cards will be arranged, followed by the test question (which is essentially all the menu items on individual cards and blank cards for the participants to write on if they wish) and the test outcome (which is how the participant actually arranges the cards).

Telling part of the story

Good quantitative metrics can certainly tell you a lot about your ROI, but it can only get you so far in understanding the full picture of what your users are experiencing, and where and why they might fall short in a product flow.

There are many more ways than those described here to collect this type of data, and we can even make up our own as we go. All that really matters is that we're measuring metrics that are relevant to our questions and that take into account the greater context of the business goal. We should also have the resources to collect and analyze this data—with awareness of our biases—and validate our findings through complementary methods.

Remember too that all of these tests come with overhead. Planning, design, engineering, and data analysis go into running and making use of them. That's certainly not a reason *not* to use them! But do take those costs into consideration when summing up the overall ROI for a project. When deciding what's worth testing while working through the KAPOW framework, factor in the effort of the test itself.

Not all of what we do can be summed up in numbers, which is why, to paint the full picture and communicate with business stakeholders the impact we have on business goals, we need to complement our quantitative proof with qualitative proof.

QUALITATIVE METRICS

To measure and communicate the impact of UXW, it's important to cross-reference quantitative methods, which tell us *what* users are doing, with qualitative methods, which tell us *why* they're doing it. Knowing why a user is or isn't taking a certain action helps focus and guide the solutions we articulate, prioritize, and implement, so that we're not wasting resources or taking a shot in the dark.

As with quantitative metrics, the first step is to decide what the goal is and what proxy can be measured to determine whether success is achieved. The research itself can be a bit expensive and time-consuming. Recruitment is somewhat trickier, and certain methods pair well (or not so well) with certain questions. Here are some popular examples.

Interviews

Talking to your users is probably the most obvious qualitative research method.

Pros and cons of interviews:

- **Pros:** Interviews are richer in insight than any other method available.
- **Cons:** It's harder to reach more than anecdotal conclusions, though a few anecdotes are often enough to signal a direction for your copy. Interviews can also be hard to recruit for, and they're time-consuming to conduct and analyze. Because of the anecdotal nature and inherent selection bias of interviews, it's important to always cross-reference findings with additional qualitative approaches.

In the project mentioned in Chapter 1, where I wanted to understand how copy impacted the perceived trustworthiness of the product, the information garnered from interviews was priceless. Whereas with other methods I could ask users to compare and contrast different trust elements, it was the interview content that generated entirely new elements that I wouldn't have thought to try on my own.

"Do these logos make you feel more or less comfortable than testimonials?" was something I could ask in a survey, but in an interview, users could tell me about how the answer "depends on *which* logos." In a survey, I could ask whether users had positive or negative feelings about testimonials, but in an interview, users could tell me *which* types of testimonials made an impact—and mention that links to third-party certifications would actually be more impactful than logos and testimonials combined. Without interviews, I may never have thought to consider third-party links. Letting users write for and with us is always mind-blowing in the best way.

Open text surveys

This type of survey is usually multiple choice or in some other format that's easy to quantify. When anyone in an organization is running a quantitative survey—usually marketing or product marketing—it's a good idea to slip in some open text questions. For example, when asking users to select which version of a screen they prefer, *A* or *B*, also ask what *about* their preferred version resonates with them and whether they can think of a third version that would work even better.

Pros and cons of open text surveys:

- **Pros:** Tests are easier to recruit for than interviews and cost less in participant compensation.
- **Cons:** Results will be more work to analyze than those from quantitative surveys and less robust than those from interviews, but they'll strike a middle ground where it's possible to get a little less insight for a little less investment of time and energy.

Adding a one-question survey to the product is a quick and inexpensive way to get a read on it (e.g., "Where did you hear about us"). We can also run one-click, multiple-choice surveys on LinkedIn and Twitter, or on other platforms where the product's audiences hang out. This is such a low-friction way to collect data that we should be able to collect a lot, quickly, from a wide range of users. Also, looking at percentages (not just absolute numbers) can tell us whether there's a shift to word-of-mouth user acquisition. If there is, we've succeeded, and our marketing department will be thrilled at the implications of their *customer acquisition cost* (CAC).

Pro tip: make the last question in the survey "Can we reach out if we have follow-up questions later?" to start collecting a list of warm leads for your next round of interviews.

Usability testing

When we test for usability, we record the screens of participants as they go through an automated set of tasks and talk us through their thought process. I've applied a lot of user testing in my work, primarily on the subscription platform UserTesting. It's an efficient way to get a lot of users to answer the "what" and "why" questions. Though participants may not be a perfect representation of your user base, they're more representative than your teammates. If you set your selection criteria carefully, recruit enough participants so that outlier feedback is not given too much weight, and analyze the results critically, you can get plenty of valuable information at a low cost, saving you from investing in the wrong direction later.

Usually, we prepare multiple versions of a static screen we're considering, an interactive prototype of a project we're midway through designing, or a live website. We ask users to complete tasks and voice their opinions, verbally and/or in writing, documenting it all.

Pros and cons of usability testing:

- **Pros:**
    - Users can be recruited and compensated quickly through various user testing platforms. For instance, you can set up a test in the evening, go to bed, and in the morning have twenty or more responses waiting. You can then spend the rest of the day listening to, reading, and analyzing the results.
    - Usability testing is less susceptible to leading questions than surveys. You get to hear users' train of thought, which can raise insights you never would've hit on with more focused survey questions.
    - You can collect quantitative and qualitative results at the same time: qualitative, from listening to participants' real and complete feedback, including their thought process, opinions, and suggestions; and quantitative, because you can count things like how many participants correctly named a product, or the number of seconds it took for them to locate an element in the navigation. On one website I tested, there were three ways to search, and my team and I measured how many of them the participants were able to identify, which they iden-

tified first, and which they preferred—as determined by which they opted to use in looking for a blog post.

- Another plus (which adds nothing to data collection, analysis, or insight but still imparts incredible value) is that live recordings have a huge, visceral impact on stakeholders and other decision-makers. When we're trying to make a point about a copy choice, backup in the participants' own words is powerful.

- **Cons:**
  - As mentioned above, user testing participants will likely not be your actual users. This can be helpful if being a user familiar with your product will bias responses—for example, if your company is trying out a new logo that existing users are anchored to but nonusers are looking at with fresh eyes. Generally, however, testing non-users is less relevant and means we have to think critically about how to interpret the results.
  - Participants in this kind of testing are being compensated and therefore may be inclined to give the responses they think the tester is looking for instead of their honest opinions.
  - When running usability testing on actual users of the product, keep in mind the bias of newer users versus older users. Older users may not expose as many usability issues because they've come to rely on workarounds discovered over time. That said, these workarounds may also be leads for tweaks you should make to your product, so try to get a sampling of users from all different segments.

In my research about the trustworthiness of a bank connect touchpoint within a flow (**FIG 1.4**), my user testing participants knew nothing about the brand. They were looking at the copy in a vacuum, whereas real users would have an association with the brand that affects how trustworthy each screen feels in important ways. On the other hand, real users had already experienced this touchpoint when they onboarded, so they were anchored to that version and therefore a biased group.

No cohort was perfect here, so we used what we had and were careful about how we synthesized our learnings.

It's a good idea to screen participants and determine whether they use similar products in their everyday lives. If the answer is yes, their preferences about your product may be influenced by conventions they've gotten used to elsewhere. You may have a far more usable experience than a competitor, but that won't register with someone who has become familiar with and accepting of "the harder version."

Cloze tests and highlighter tests

We can think of cloze tests as being kind of like Mad Libs, showing users copy but leaving some words out (**FIG 4.8**). They can help with naming a product, describing the value proposition of a feature, and puzzling out other scenarios. When we just can't put our finger on the exact word we need, or when there's an internal disagreement between synonyms, we can ask the user what makes sense to them.

Pros and cons of cloze tests:

- **Pros:** A cloze test lets you ask the same participant many questions, and since recruitment can be a major research challenge, it's a great opportunity to get a lot of data at once. It may also open the team's eyes to copy possibilities they might never have come up with on their own. This is especially useful if there's an internal debate about terms they can't settle—like whether a credit card fee should be called a "transaction fee" or "processing fee." Cloze findings could show an overwhelming majority of participants find "interchange fee" to be the most natural descriptor.
- **Cons:** We won't be using participants' copy verbatim, as it might not match the product voice and tone or meet industry conventions. Also, it's more important with cloze tests to recruit participants from our target population who have some knowledge and context for the product, features, flows, and value.

More time to pay	Repayments your way
Gain confidence that your most important expenses can be paid on time.	Get 3 extra business days to repay—with no fees when you pay by ACH or debit card, or a small _____ fee when you pay by credit card.	Repay within the 3-day grace period or the outstanding amount will automatically continue as a _____ on your credit line.

Peace of mind
Confidence and control

Transaction
Processing
Interchange

Loan
Draw
Balance

FIG 4.8: Cloze tests can validate copy choices as well as open our eyes to entirely new directions for copy. Sometimes, letting users write their own copy is best.

If cloze tests ask participants to fill in the blanks, highlighter tests show us what they think of the words already on the page. Tell users to highlight what they don't understand, or to use certain colors for words that they feel support them through a specific flow in-product.

Social media feedback

Say our business goal is to increase product reputation. We do the user research to inform our hypotheses about what kind of copy changes would address shortcomings in the product's current reputation. It could be something small, like users feeling that tasks take too long because the copy doesn't walk them through each step clearly enough. We focus on the highest-volume flows—or the most sensitive, or those most vulnerable to giving users a bad impression—and rewrite the copy so it's clearer. Then we check in with users again, asking, "Do we have a reputation for being a comfortable, convenient, easy to use—even delightful—product?"

But wait. How do we measure reputation in the first place?

One way is to look at what people are saying about the product on social media. If the app is for bookworms, join their Facebook groups to see what they're saying there. They're likely more honest with one another than they would be with you if you recruited them to join a research session.

What do ratings look like on the customer review website Trustpilot (**FIG 4.9**)? The site has a star system of course, but it also has free text comments. Quantitative insights given in a

Oct 20, 2017

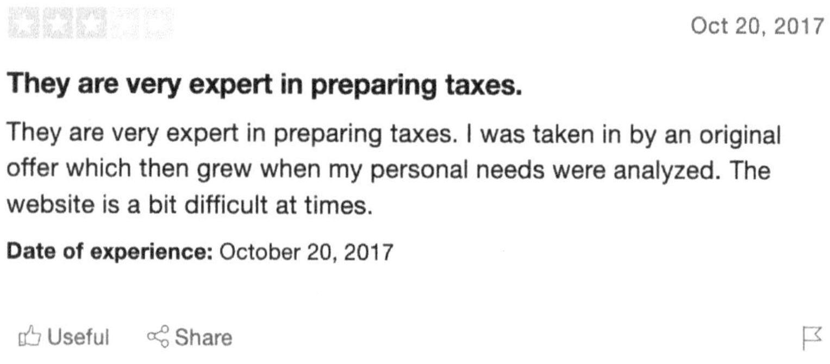

They are very expert in preparing taxes.

They are very expert in preparing taxes. I was taken in by an original offer which then grew when my personal needs were analyzed. The website is a bit difficult at times.

Date of experience: October 20, 2017

👍 Useful   ⤳ Share   ⚑

FIG 4.9: Trustpilot allows customers to leave both quantitative and qualitative reviews, creating a more comprehensive view of feedback.

vacuum will never be as robust as their qualitative counterparts. A product may have a lot of low ratings, but if it turns out that the reason is because it's a tax app and users hate taxes...well, I wouldn't quite take that as a failure. Likewise, if a product has high ratings because it recently ran a promotion, that's not particularly useful in our mission as UX writers.

Obviously, scouring sites and digging into free-text comments is more labor-intensive than running a script that takes automatic measurements and spits out numbers. But you should get some consolation from the fact that you don't need nearly as many participants. Once patterns start to emerge, you should be able to draw reliable and actionable conclusions pretty fast.

Telling the whole story

There are many ways to measure success, and sometimes the hardest part is deciding which to use. Qualitative testing contextualizes the big, impressive numbers that come out of quantitative measurements, rounding out the story of the product and the success of its copy into something we can build on. As methods, both work best when combined.

Good qualitative data requires the establishment of relevant metrics, the use of cost-efficient tools and approaches for taking measurements, accurate interpretation of the results, and the distilling of those results into actionable insights. There are "right" methods for each situation, based on the copy under investigation and the resources available—some of which can be captured in the wild for free. Some qualitative research won't result in tangible deliverables (like assessing how ethical an experience is), but it still shouldn't be ignored. UXW has a positive impact on the business and users in ways that can't always be quantified; nevertheless, those aspects are extremely valuable.

Research-based copy is possible, and it can be done well if we leverage all of the resources at our disposal and work together to critically analyze our thinking, challenge our biases, and execute on our decisions.

THINKING BIGGER

As UX writers we need to start thinking *beyond*—beyond the user to the business, and beyond creating copy to measuring its success. We should think beyond product copy, too—we have the potential to make a much broader impact if we do. Broader impact means more opportunities for leveling up and specializing, and more reason to increase our team's head count.

5

IMPACTING THE BUSINESS BEYOND UX WRITING

WRITING MICROCOPY IS LARGELY TACTICAL. It's about getting down to the finest resolution, the copy version of getting the experience "pixel perfect." It's amazing how each "pixel" can have such an impact on the user experience—and by extension, the business's success—but it's not the only way we can contribute.

UX writers are usually working at a ratio of one writer to two-to-ten times as many designers and product managers, which means we spend a lot of our time writing microcopy for products and features being developed for the first time and updating them later as needed. If we can get ahead of the game in that department, we can zoom out and do more strategic work that—while harder to quantify—will make a big impact on the business. A lot of this work involves improving efficiency for the business and will be felt more indirectly by the users, but as we've covered earlier, improvements for either generally mean greater success for both.

When I'm asked what we UX writers do all day, I do explain microcopy, which is something so many people take for granted, not realizing there's a dedicated person behind the curtain putting thought into every character. But I also explain that some of the most challenging and fun things we do include content ops, voice and tone work, conversation design, and workflow management—all of which serves the business in profound ways.

CONTENT OPS

Content operations (content ops) is the non-user-facing element of a UX writer's work. This work is done entirely inside the organization; the user will never see the deliverables. Though the business will likely benefit the fastest, as internal optimization saves resources (which can then be reallocated), content ops, when done right, will also save users from inconsistencies, delays, and other headaches through the very same work that makes the business more efficient. Just as improving usability for some (through accessibility measures) improves usability for all, efficiency for the business creates a better experience for the users (https://bkaprt.com/buxw43/05-01).

Content documentation

The depth and breadth of the work we do—paired with our usually small size as a team—means documentation and process are crucial. Owning content ops means, among other things, managing the documentation of copy iterations, inconsistencies, decisions, and an "inventory" of strings in production. There are new tools emerging to replace Google Docs and Sheets for these tasks; many integrate directly with design programs and code, giving writers end-to-end control over copy to streamline updates and save resources.

Owning content ops might be more natural for UX writers who have autonomy beyond the tactical writing of microcopy. Either way, I recommend that every UX writer talk to their manager about taking responsibility for a part of their team's operations. For example, there should be no objection to any UX writer taking the initiative to investigate new tools as they come out, doing the preliminary research to decide whether any are useful to the company. That writer may not make the final decision about whether a tool is introduced, but their role as a "new tool radar" is good for their own professional development and the greater team's efficiency.

Organization-wide education

Content ops also involves educating the company about UXW on an organized level. For instance, we can create onboarding modules around voice and tone for new employees; run regular, live, interdepartmental workshops for individual contributors who write user-facing copy; and set time aside to answer questions about "how this whole copy thing works." Education is a great outlet for expressing our passion for what we do, and that excitement will rub off on other teams until collaboration is more fun and productive for everyone.

Content processes

Another aspect of content ops is creating and optimizing content processes. For example, a business stakeholder where I worked came up with new incentives and products to offer users to increase the business's revenue. However, content people were getting feedback from that team too late and too indirectly. I started a mini-process with two touchpoints between the business and content stakeholders: the first I called a Language Kickoff, and the second, to be held about a week after the first, a Language Check-In.

1. **The Language Kickoff** is meant to take place before the first bits of copy are drafted and strongly resembles user research. As writers, our expertise lies in communicating with the user, not in understanding the business considerations going on behind the scenes. During the Kickoff, we writers essentially sit back and listen to the business stakeholders talk about their new initiative. What is it? What's the internal and external context? What audience segments will be eligible? What parts of the initiative do they expect to resonate with those target audiences? As they talk, we take

notes on the language they're using, jotting down quotes as well as summaries. Then we set off to draft copy.

2. **The Language Check-in** is where we show business stakeholders a sample of what we've drafted. This is meant to be a sort of course correction; the stakeholders can see how we implemented the things we learned and confirm whether we understood them correctly. (Chances are we got some of it right and some of it wrong.) After that, we head off to write the rest of the copy and don't run it by them again. Really, we don't. Lots of stakeholders will have their hands on the copy as it matures, including product managers, compliance officers, and others. The business stakeholders need to step out before then, to avoid a "too many cooks in the content" situation.

This short and simple two-step process meant that we content folk could get context and terminology directly (allowing us to ask questions) and early (so that we wouldn't have to backtrack later and update misplaced or misused terms). We saved time, gave everyone involved clarity on sources of truth, and collectively gained a better handle on version control. The iteration that happened in these live sessions meant less was needed in asynchronous forums like Google Doc comment threads, making collaboration far more efficient and pleasant. Business stakeholders felt listened to and proactive while content processes continued smoothly, with just the right amount of stakeholder involvement.

Managing content processes, creating them if none exist, and checking in regularly to keep them useful and up-to-date—this is all part of content ops.

Content practice scalability

Scalable practices also fall under content ops. For example, I led the copy guild at my organization. We managed a Google Drive folder where copy docs were shared across the company and established best practices for granting permissions. This not only saved people from having to ask where stuff was kept—and waiting for access requests to be answered—but it also safe-guarded scalability in the face of inevitable personnel changes.

We created a *content style guide* (CSG) and hosted it on an internal website with a convenient *content management system* (CMS) on the backend. Workshops were held to get content creators throughout the organization on board. Other tasks included managing the CSG's permissions, maintaining the CMS, onboarding team members, and owning ongoing train-ing. Ownership here is critical; if we UX writers don't do it, no one else will. Between the amount of time and energy saved, the number of internal users empowered, and the increased consistency of the user experience, it's well worth the effort.

In this case, I also implemented a tool called Writer (https://bkaprt.com/buxw43/05-02), which works like Grammarly (https://bkaprt.com/buxw43/05-03) but for internal guidelines. As part of my content ops role, I did the research to choose the tool, worked with many cross-disciplinary teams to get the appropriate permissions and integrations set up, managed the licenses, trained team members on how to use it, and took responsibility for its maintenance. I also tracked metrics on an ongoing basis to decide whether to reallocate licenses and whether to renew/upgrade the contract each year.

Systemic organization of content documentation, CSG devel-opment, structured education, and automation tools are all pieces in the scalability element of content ops.

Rallying the troops

It can be hard for us content people to let go of the words. They're our babies, and we want to coddle each and every one. But that's not scalable. And we're not scalable. Writers are people, too. No matter how much head count we finagle, in a healthy and growing business there will always be more content than we can manage.

That's why an important part of our job is to empower con-tent creators outside of the copy guild. There are several ways we can do this:

- Create and distribute a CSG with supportive training materials—an excellent first step in getting content creators from every department on the same page.
- Seek out tools that automate its implementation, like Writer, and spread licenses across departments.
- Regularly host workshops and respond to feedback on the style guidelines and tools. This will make content creators real partners in leveling up every written word the business puts out into the world.

You can't be everywhere, but your standards can.

We should also aim to get all stakeholders to care that copy is done right. I can't count the number of internal talks and workshops I've given to inspire non-content creators to use their power to support our practice.

I know it's working because I've had engineers come to me and brag about how they found a Readability Guideline violation in the code—and updated it all on their own. Compliance officers have flagged content from non-writers and insisted it go through the copy guild for review before entering the regulatory approval pipeline. Product managers have been unwilling to update the smallest, most obvious, in-product copy corrections without a copy guild member's official signoff. Designers have been unwilling to finalize elements with proto-copy still in place.

When we instill a deep appreciation for UXW in everyone around us, the business benefits, as do the users and the entire content practice. Empowering content-adjacent partners is just another part of our responsibility as UX writers who own content ops.

VOICE AND TONE

Voice and tone are two of our more obvious responsibilities. This work includes development, documentation, distribution, and quality control. Voice and tone also need to evolve as the company, brand, and user segments evolve.

Voice and tone development

Before anyone can align on voice and tone, there needs to be some kind of established intent (similar to a business goal). I'd recommend digging around to see if there are any voice writing principles out there already. If not, talk to longtime employees about how the product voice has evolved over their tenure, and ask founders or executives to share whatever visions they have or have had in this area. Also, investigate the marketing department. While marketing copy differs from product copy in tone, the two need to jibe—otherwise we risk presenting a jarringly inconsistent personality to the user.

Regardless of whether voice and tone already exist, we have work to do. We need to review whatever material is available and determine if it meets our current goals. Be prepared to expand and reformat if necessary, or even start from scratch. The success of this process comes down to multiple factors, like working with stakeholders to determine the personality of the brand, creating or reevaluating user personas, and writing high-level guidelines that define how the conversation between our brand and our users should sound. For a tactical step-by-step guide for developing voice and tone, I recommend reading *Microcopy: The Complete Guide*, by Kinneret Yifrah.

Voice and tone are an important foundation for good UXW, but they're not enough. The next level of resolution is a style guide. Like voice and tone, style guides address development, documentation, distribution, and quality control for brand language.

Style guides are the nitty-gritty of the voice and tone guide. Here's where we dive into our company's policy on capitalization (e.g., whether to use title case or sentence case on buttons), spaces around em dashes, British versus American English (or a parallel decision in other languages), date formatting, and more. Some of these decisions reflect the voice; for instance, if a pillar of our product voice is to be conversational, our style guide might call for the use of positive contractions. Other decisions have little to do with expressing our voice and simply need to be documented for the sake of consistency, such as whether to use periods after abbreviated months (*Jan.* versus *Jan*).

Internally, it's important to have a source of truth to align with, because the user should be interacting with a product—not with a marketing team, product team, UX team, or engineering team. Our communications need to be cohesive and consistent, reflecting a single personality: the product's.

I want to emphasize the value of crowdsourcing improvements and leveraging new eyes. Every person who uses the product voice and tone should be thinking about them critically and suggesting adjustments from their perspective.

Some of the most valuable changes I've made have come from support and sales representatives who talk to users every day and are in a better position than I am to say which terms resonate and which don't. Marketers, who spend more time analyzing the competition than I do, can make important contributions about how language in the industry is changing and advise us on what we can do to keep up. Everyone is responsible for keeping an ear to the ground and fostering the product voice and tone.

Guideline documentation

Once we've gone through the process of developing voice and tone, we need to get the final decisions down on (virtual) paper. We'll have collected a lot of opinions by this point—some conflicting—and we'll have been through a number of iterations. It's important to document the final (for now) guidelines, knowing life and words are dynamic and will continue to evolve as the product, users, and market do.

Think through what to include in your voice and tone documentation:

- Rules of thumb
- Specific examples
- Links to how decisions were made
- References to validate best practices
- Contact information for questions and feedback

My current company's style guide includes guardrails and examples: a simpler model. However, there's also an emphasis

FIG 5.1: Mailchimp's content style guide is publicly available and an excellent example to follow (bkaprt.com/05-04).

FIG 5.2: Fundbox's content style guide was modeled after Mailchimp's. Fundbox doesn't maintain a public version, but this image should give you a good idea of what it's like.

on input; the managers of the guide have written information on how to reach us if anyone has questions or wants to suggest edits.

Think about how to format and publish your documentation, whether in a Google Doc, Confluence page, website, or something else. We took inspiration from Mailchimp's public content style guide (**FIG 5.1**) for both our formatting and the decision to have our guide live on an internal website (**FIG 5.2**).

Our content style guide website is easy to navigate and share. We integrated with Okta, an access management company, because it doesn't require manual permissions, giving easy and reliable access to everyone at the company. When it came time to introduce the style guide, we opted for a workshop format; teams learned the *who, what, when, where, why,* and—most importantly—*how* of using it. Unlike Mailchimp's, our guide isn't publicly available. (This is what worked for us; every business will have its own considerations. There's no right answer, so long as it works.)

A CMS on the backend lets the CSG managers make edits and updates quickly without engineering or other dependencies. In any format, the documentation needs to be agile. It's important to constantly and proactively gather feedback and iterate accordingly, because the product, user base, and market are not static things. User-facing teams—who speak with the users every day, such as those in sales and support—may have invaluable insight into how we can produce accurate and useful voice and tone documentation. We need to make integrating such insights—and generally being flexible—part of our process.

I've led the effort with strong support from the marketing copywriter. We're the ones with CMS access, and we're the ones responsible for staying updated on the latest evidence and making decisions when changes need to be made. We're also responsible for distribution—getting the information to the right teams, at the right time, and in the right way—as well as for researching and implementing tools like Writer that make the application of voice and tone easier and more consistent.

Voice and tone distribution and education

So, whom do we share the documentation with?

First and foremost: the marketing and product teams. These were most likely the teams that led the effort to create and document voice and tone in the first place, so they already have skin in the game.

After the marketing and product teams, we share our work with anyone else creating user-facing communications, starting with sales and support reps.

Last but certainly not least, we loop in teams who create external, non-user-facing communications, such as corporate communications, public relations, and business development teams. The more use cases we have to stress-test our guide, and the more eyes we have providing feedback, the better it will become, improving the experience for users and the solidity of the business's brand.

What education should be provided along with the documentation we share? We can't just blast an email to the entire company and expect anything to actually happen. There are a few things we can do:

- **Build interactive online modules** (there are many programs available to help with this!) and assign them to existing employees, as well as to new employees as part of their onboarding process.
- **Deliver live workshops** with individual teams where you introduce the product voice and tone, with or without interactive exercises that let them try it on for size while you're right there to help.
- **Record educational sessions** and send them out afterward for participants to reference later, including any team members who couldn't attend.

There are lots of creative ways to get our product's voice and tone in front of the right people, aided by educational tools that help them help you apply it for the sake of the users and business. Planning and executing the distribution of voice and tone is a critical yet often-overlooked part of a UX writer's role.

Quality control

After launching the product's voice and tone with documentation and education, we have to make sure they're applied consistently and comprehensively: *quality control.* This may mean (at least at the start) setting up a process where all new communications are reviewed or spot-checked by the voice and tone owners; alternatively, automation tools like Writer may be implemented. Depending on the size and maturity of the organization—and our bandwidth as UX writers—we may want to provide additional training for ambassadors on different teams, tasking them with keeping watch over the communications coming out of their respective departments.

Quality control means making sure everyone knows where to bring their questions and ideas, and that these are listened to. We have a Slack channel for this purpose; the questions and ideas we receive often inspire updates to the CSG. We should also be keeping an eye on live communications—in-product and in other materials—to catch anything that slips through the cracks before launch, or to open tickets for correcting errors retroactively.

It's not enough to create a voice; it's the UX writer's job to follow through to the end and ensure that the voice comes alive.

CONVERSATION DESIGN

Traditional UIs require users to interact through a screen. But what if a voice interface allowed them to engage while driving or watching their kids in the park? What would that mean for their success with the product and, in turn, for the success of the business? Could increasing access points to a product mean extra exposure for existing features—more bang for your buck? Is it worth investing in?

Conversation design, which includes writing voice interfaces and conversations for chatbots, opens up a multitude of opportunities. In businesses where voice interfaces and chatbots don't exist, UX writers can do the research and estimate the potential ROI of introducing them, both by understanding the impact on the user and the impact on the business. Is it worth it for both sides? This research will need to be incredibly thorough—and it'll have very technical elements—but that doesn't mean the UX writer should not lead it. If we don't, no one likely will. We're the owners of the language experience, and that includes voice and chatbot interactions, even if they don't (yet) exist. While investigating the potential of conversational design elements, UX writers should build out a plan for implementation, maintenance, optimization, and scale. For more, I recommend Erika Hall's book *Conversational Design*.

Chatbots

Ever since Facebook opened Messenger for chatbots in 2016, they've been widely adopted by digital products everywhere. Chatbots are basically software that simulates human conversations with users by SMS (text messages to your phone) or by a text chat widget inside the app. On desktop, they usually look like a word bubble on the bottom right corner of the screen (https://bkaprt.com/buxw43/05-05).

Chatbots are helpful for users because they're faster and more available than human reps, and they're great for businesses because they can respond to users more simultaneously—cheap (basically free) scalability. While chatbots do rely on reps for escalation when the designed conversation fails, far fewer reps are needed because the bot is screening the highest volume of inquiries. Good for users, good for business, and everyone's happy...but the UX writer still needs to make it happen.

Owning a chatbot requires far more than just writing; it means doing a lot of research to understand what types of scripts will catch the highest volume of user inquiries. You'll also have to:

- Design flows using any of the many prototyping tools out there
- Understand the technical implementation requirements in order to prioritize the conversations to implement

- Choose analytic tools and establish a process for applying learnings in every interaction of the bot
- Collaborate with support reps who receive the bot escalations
- Actually write the text

To learn more, I recommend following Hillary Black, on any platform (https://bkaprt.com/buxw43/05-06).

Voice user interfaces

Voice user interfaces (VUIs)—like Siri, Google Assistant, and Alexa—let users interact with digital products through verbal commands. Primary advantages of VUIs include the eyes-free experience that's critical for driving; the hands-free experience necessary while cooking or holding a baby; and accessibility for users with visual impairments, to name a few.

A major challenge with VUIs is discoverability—how do you peruse a voice app to discover features? Another is privacy—what about interactions that are broadcast out loud but contain sensitive information, like medical or financial data (https://bkaprt.com/buxw43/05-07)?

Taken together, it's clear how VUIs can complement *graphical user interfaces* (GUIs). They can also remain stand-alone alternatives for some experiences, though they may not be suitable for others. We shouldn't build out a voice option because it's trendy or because we can. As always, we need to think about user needs and business goals, and whether a voice interface can help us meet them.

Assuming an organization is interested in adding a VUI element for all the right reasons, it's up to the UX writer to do it. As with chatbots, we need to own it. Even if the bulk of the work isn't writing, the writer still needs to own it. I once partnered with an engineer to create an Alexa skill for my office during an internal hackathon and was unpleasantly surprised at how few words there were to write. It's one of the reasons I decided against pursuing the conversation design specialty in my career. But for others, it's exactly the kind of work that excites and challenges them.

As the owners, we're responsible for doing the research to decide whether and how to best build the VUI, for getting the necessary buy-in to make it happen, and for managing the project and all of its moving parts—even the parts we're not doing ourselves (i.e., everything but the writing). If a VUI is right for the users and the business, it's a unique, novel, and awesome way for UX writers to impact ROI while also leveling up the user experience. For more information, I recommend checking out Preston So's *Voice Content and Usability* and Cathy Pearl's *Designing Voice User Interfaces*.

JUGGLING IT ALL

UX writers are generally hired at a low ratio compared to designers and product managers, and we're expected to write across many products and features. To do that most effectively, we need a framework for balancing our tasks. In other words, while we have KAPOW for *each* product or feature we work on, we also need a framework for managing our workload holistically across business needs.

If we get this part right, we gain a multiplier effect without adding much overhead at all. It's about working smarter, not harder. We can level up our practice and boost our overall impact by prioritizing intelligently, scoping accurately, applying automation, and offering transparency for stakeholders.

Holistic process

As UX writers, we won't always be working on initiatives of our own. A lot of readers may be thinking: "Initiating my own strategic copy improvements would be great, but I'm too busy putting out fires!" While we've talked a lot about going out and finding goals to chase, much of what we do involves fielding requests as they come in. So how do we move from being reactive to proactive?

First, we need to define an intake process for new requests. Random Slack messages or emails asking for "just one string (or six)" is *not* going to work. (Neither are shoulder taps in the hallway.) There's no one-size-fits-all solution, but whatever we decide, we need to communicate it and stick to it. Make it known that requests that don't follow the intake process will be ignored. It's not personal; it's process, and it's in place for everyone's benefit. It's the only way to guarantee that asks won't fall through the cracks and that we prioritize responses responsibly.

It also helps if task owners have visibility into what else is on our desk: for example, an Asana board with all of the current UXW tasks. They'll see exactly what we're juggling and why turnaround might be taking longer than they expected. "Show, don't tell" applies to more than just the impact of our writing.

When we're part of a team and not a lone soldier, we need a second step: from intake to triage. Let task owners know which writer has been assigned to their task so that a) they know the task has been picked up, and b) they know whom to follow up with so as not to pester the whole team.

Impact

Now that we have a process for intake, we need to decide *where* to start working. When prioritizing our to-do list, the urgency of tasks is important; but, in my opinion, impact comes first. We need to work with the task owner to understand a few things: What problem does the task solve? Is it a must-have or a nice-to-have? Is it a bug in production or a general improvement? I'm not saying nice-to-haves and general improvements shouldn't happen—of course they should—but they shouldn't be prioritized over more impactful projects.

Every task uses up time, and time is a limited resource. Every minute spent on one task comes at the expense of another. We need to make that trade-off wisely.

Urgency

Urgency might be the most obvious consideration. Is the task part of a fix for a security breach? Pop that baby to the top of the list. Is it to support a marketing campaign planned for who knows when? It can wait. There may be overlap between impact and urgency; for example, a security breach will have major negative impact on the business and should be fixed immediately for damage control.

To start triaging according to deadlines, we need deadlines. ASAP is not a deadline. Let task owners know that specifying deadlines is a requirement for the intake process, and anything labeled "ASAP" will board the express train to the bottom of the list.

Sometimes, owners won't know how to define their deadline, and we can help. Ask what the task is blocking, what dependencies the task has, and what the timeline is for those to be resolved. If the task is blocking roll-out of a major roadmap feature, then we'll need the launch date of the roll-out to accurately assess the urgency. This information may not be available right away. If that's the case, we'll need to find out when it will be and factor that into the triage. Say the task owner only needs a day but can't start until the product team finalizes the spec; the clock doesn't have to start ticking yet. We can actually leverage dependencies by scheduling other tasks into the moments we find ourselves waiting. Multitasking at its finest.

Even if owners think they have a deadline, we should question it. I'm not accusing owners of padding their deadlines (though it has been known to happen). What I am suggesting is that owners aren't always intimately familiar with our process; they aren't necessarily the right person to estimate how long we'll need to complete the task. I've had owners tell me they need something quickly, only to realize on my own that I didn't need to get started until the following sprint. Others told me there was plenty of time—three whole days—for a task that would take me at least twice as long. The latter often happens because non-writers aren't always aware that the shorter the text, the longer it can take to get it right, as a general rule.

Because "fast" is subjective, we need to keep asking questions until we get an answer concrete enough to be lined up against everything else we've got going on.

Scope

While we're having that conversation about realistic timelines, we also need to nail down scope: the size of the task. Owners are usually unaware of how much time goes into a copy task—and that's okay. We just need to keep asking questions until we figure it out.

I've been asked for five hundred words, which the owner assumed would take days, when the truth was I had so much evergreen content to lean on that I scoped it at about an hour. I've also been asked for a ten-word error validation that the owner assumed was a matter of minutes, but once I drilled down into the various states, segments, and entry points, I corrected as two days.

Owners do not dictate scope. Only we as UX writers have the tools and experience to scope accurately, and when we manage expectations—including our own—everyone benefits. To prioritize tasks, we need to know how big they are. If we have a high-impact task with a very big scope, for example, and another with less impact but that can be banged out in an hour, we'll probably want to get the smaller task out of the way first. There's no "first come, first served" in copy tasks. We're following a matrix of factors that tells us where it makes the most sense to begin, and on and on.

Once, when I was brand-new to UXW, a PM asked me for a copy task. He gave me a deadline, and soon I realized I wasn't going to make it. I panicked. I consulted another PM who told me I had no reason to panic at all; apparently, the first PM shouldn't have given me a deadline but rather asked me to scope the task myself. I should've been the one to give the (more accurate) estimation, and if my estimate was too long, the PM could choose to scope down the ask. After that pep talk, I walked up to the first PM, told him what I could do by his date and by what date I could do it all, and asked if I should deliver later or deliver less. He chose later and totally took it in stride. I had nothing to worry about at all. Scope is never set in stone, and only open communication between domain experts will produce an accurate assessment.

Automation

All of these tips are built on the assumption that we're human. But what if we weren't human? Or rather, what if we were augmented via scalable automation tools? For example, if we integrated a plugin that would automatically correct style guide inconsistencies, stakeholders would be better equipped to bring cleaner drafts, saving everyone time. Between an accessible, easy-to-use, and comprehensive style guide and a plugin—Writer—I've been able to cut out a lot of the work that copy people used to do. Of course, these tools can't replace talented humans, but they can grab the low-hanging fruit so we can focus on more complicated areas.

Doing the work—gathering research, getting approval, installing, distributing, training, and maintaining tools—will take time away from other tasks, but it will pay for itself many-fold in the currency of time. We should always look for ways to make task-ticking faster and better, overall.

Transparency and communication

Whatever our intake process and however we define urgency and scope, through it all we need to communicate, communicate, communicate. The more transparency task owners have regarding our process and progress, the more they'll feel like partners, respect our time, and be satisfied with the deliverables. We should never be a black box—we should be a fish tank.

Personal interactions

In my experience, personal interactions tend to have the greatest impact on communication. We might run a workshop for all content creators on how to use the style guide when we roll it out. We could crash a product team's daily sync (going through the proper channels to get on the agenda first) to walk everyone through our intake process, using visuals for each step (e.g., on an Asana board)—all the way through to when and how they can expect updates and deliverables.

When someone's not getting it, don't be afraid to reach out directly and ask what's not working for them. Be genuinely open to hearing suggestions that can lower the barrier to entry for stakeholders; what good is a process if it doesn't work for everyone? We all want the same thing—to get work done in the smoothest possible way—so we need to collaborate to make that happen. Cracking a whip on anyone who doesn't follow exactly what we laid out is not going to be effective. If we're agile and open to other perspectives, we'll build a process that results in the best outcomes.

Documented requirements

Documenting requirements is an excellent way to communicate across disciplines. This can come in many forms: a brief from a business stakeholder to a product manager; a *product requirements document* (PRD) from a product manager to a UX team; a Jira epic from product managers to engineers, and so on.

Requirements don't contain the solution, but they do contain everything the next team needs to develop a solution. That said, receiving requirements doesn't mean we're being told what to do; it's a conversation. We don't have to accept the requirements without question, and as a best practice, we shouldn't. Even in the case of adding copy, we shouldn't get down to work before getting complete context. Here are some questions to ask (if receiving requirements) or answer (if writing up documentation):

- Why is this needed from a business perspective? Or is it a regulatory concern?
- Why is this needed from a user perspective (which we discovered through our user-facing teams)?
- Why is this needed from a product perspective? Has there been a change in functionality?
- What are our limitations in solving this problem, technical and otherwise?
- What is our timeframe for delivery?
- How should this task be prioritized against other projects on our plate?

Requirements include all of the information the product manager assumes we need—yet they don't necessarily know what we need. This is our opportunity to help them help us.

HUDDLE UP

The business of UXW goes beyond microcopy. Content ops, voice and tone, conversation design, and prioritization across the organization all bring additional layers of impact on the user experience and on the business.

UXW is not meant to be done in a vacuum. In fact, it's the opposite: it may be one of the most collaborative roles in an entire organization. To do our jobs well, we need to have smooth working relationships and clear processes in place for collaborating with cross-disciplinary teammates.

This can only happen if we start calling each other *teammates* and recognizing that UX writers and business stakeholders (and users) want the same thing: to succeed. By communicating verbally and often, providing clear documentation, and being transparent about our processes, workloads, and priorities, we elevate these relationships to peak functionality—to everyone's benefit.

Now this is not the end. It is not even the beginning of the end. But it is, perhaps, the end of the beginning.
—SIR WINSTON CHURCHILL

UXW HAS COME A LONG way from not having a name to having a proper seat at the table—but we can't stop now. We're at a critical moment in the development of our field, and only we can decide where to take it next. We've passed infancy, where we had no real shape or plan; passed toddlerhood, where we got our basic footing but were still completely disorganized; passed the early teens, where we threw tantrums about needing to be heard. We are now young adults. We are thoughtful and productive, having come so far from the drooling blob we used to be—but we have far to go. Now is when we decide which road to take through the biggest part of our lives, where we'll leave our biggest mark on the world.

It's time for us to specialize. We've codified general rules of thumb and formalized general models, which is a great (and necessary) starting point. But now it's time to drill down and get smarter, more sophisticated, and more advanced. We should be heading toward a world where UX writers specialize in B2B or B2C as product managers often do; we should have accessibility, inclusivity, and localization UXW experts instead of expecting each of us to do it all. We should be budgeting real research time into our process, and we *should* get that time because it's a fundamental part of doing our work well.

Most importantly, we UX writers need to rethink our role relative to the overall business. We've been advocating for the user for so long (because we had to!) that we've lost sight of what makes the product world turn: a whole ecosystem that includes the users and the creators of the product they're using. We often start from the conditioned position that user and business needs must clash fundamentally; but in truth, they are each other's most important partner. I hope we can shift our tone and approach from a combative fire-putting-out vibe to a calmer, zoomed-out one where we see ourselves as part of a much bigger picture. For one thing, it would help us understand how "better" copy doesn't always mean that which more closely adheres to a UXW rule of thumb, but rather that which better achieves shared business goals.

We need greater emphasis on collaboration—not just with our users, but with teammates across our organization. Talks at UXW conferences should discuss collaboration as well as craft. How do we listen so stakeholders will talk? How do we get the greatest context possible from the business and turn it into greater copy? How do we get the most out of working with other domain experts? In other words, how do we succeed, together?

It all starts with clear communication. We must be able to understand the business and its goals, even when no one else does (yet). We must be able to explain what we need in order to help the business reach those goals. We must show results quickly and clearly in units of measurement that the business works in, and we must do so across multiple product units at the same time. KAPOW, the framework for the ROI of UXW, is a great place to start. After that, it's time to analyze the quantitative and qualitative measures of what we achieved with KAPOW. Finally, we level up, hitting business goals that go beyond copy through content ops and management.

I wrote this book in the hope that we might start UXW's young adulthood together, because we're hardly at the beginning of the end. We're more at the end of the beginning—and specialization, collaboration, and an emphasis on the business side of the user-product partnership are the newest tools for our success.

ACKNOWLEDGMENTS

THANK YOU TO Katel LeDû and Lisa Maria Marquis at A Book Apart for giving me a chance to fulfill the dream of writing a book; Torrey Podmajersky who made me think I could; Sarah Winters who made me think I should; and Patrick Stafford who reviewed an early manuscript.

Thank you to my very first mentors, Ofer Karp and Gahl Pratt Pardes, who laid the foundation for everything I've done in the UXW world.

Thank you to my team at Fundbox: Naama Hirsh, Shir Lavi, Shiran Birenbaum, Sonia Sheinman, and Noa Saroya, and especially Michal Simkovits, who designs everything I present to the world (including images in this book), and Nadav Yaron, mentor of a lifetime.

Thank you to my husband, Josh, and kids Maya, Adelle, and Ori, who keep me focused on what matters.

And most of all, thank you to my grandparents, Lil and Dave Brick, Elaine and Cal Turin, and my parents Carol and Alan Brick-Turin, to whom I owe my every achievement.

RESOURCES

THERE WERE A LOT OF TEASERS in this book about juicy areas to dive into. This list of resources should help guide you to the rabbit hole of your choosing.

Books

It's hard to decide which books to read when they all look so good, and many appear similar. Here's where I would recommend beginning:

- *Accessibility for Everyone* by Laura Kalbag is an excellent place to get started with accessibility. Everyone in the industry needs working knowledge of this vast topic—start here (https://bkaprt.com/buxw43/06-01).
- *Content Design* by Sarah Winters (was Richards) is the book that coined the term. While it's not necessarily written from a product-content perspective, the insights are very relevant for how we think about our work (https://bkaprt.com/buxw43/06-03).
- *Conversational Design* by Erika Hall is mind-blowing. This is not light reading about applying best practices—it's a real think piece about how we approach writing interfaces for real people, starting with a history of human communication (https://bkaprt.com/buxw43/06-03).
- *Cultivating Content Design* by Beth Dunn is only becoming more relevant as UXW goes from being done by non-UX writers, to being done by UX writers, to being done by whole entire UXW teams as more companies recognize the value of the practice (https://bkaprt.com/buxw43/06-04).
- *Don't Make Me Think* by Steve Krug is a classic from the greater UX space. It's short and fun to read (https://bkaprt.com/buxw43/06-05).
- *Just Enough Research* by Erika Hall tears down all of the arguments against user research and explains how to get maximum ROI for the research we do (https://bkaprt.com/buxw43/06-06).

- *Letting Go of the Words* by Ginny Redish is a classic full of real-life examples and case studies (https://bkaprt.com/buxw43/06-07).
- *Microcopy: The Complete Guide* by Kinneret Yifrah provides a strong foundation for UXW tactics and heuristics (https://bkaprt.com/buxw43/06-08).
- *Presenting Design Work* by Donna Spencer is an important read because, as you've seen in this book, a huge part of what we do is communicate what we do. Presenting is a part of the job description (https://bkaprt.com/buxw43/06-09).
- *Strategic Writing for UX* by Torrey Podmajersky provides a strong foundation for UXW strategy (https://bkaprt.com/buxw43/06-10).
- *Writing is Designing* by Andy Welfe and Michael J. Metts solidifies the idea that UX writers design with words as opposed to "just write" (https://bkaprt.com/buxw43/06-11).

Conferences

While a book can only reflect a moment in time, conferences are hubs of ongoing conversation. Attending conferences is the best way to stay up to date and inspired, and to contribute to the UXW community and practice:

- Button (https://bkaprt.com/buxw43/06-12) by Brain Traffic is the biggest and best conference specifically for product writers.
- Confab (https://bkaprt.com/buxw43/06-13) covers the wider content world; unfortunately, Brain Traffic is producing it for the final time in 2023. But even if Confab is coming to an end, it pays to look up past speakers for ideas of whom to follow. You can also read takeaways and other content that was published during and after the conference each year.
- Utterly Content (https://bkaprt.com/buxw43/06-14) by Pickle Jar Communications covers all things content through global, virtual attendance.

Podcasts

"I heard a podcast about that!" is my famous catchphrase at work—and for good reason. Just ask any of the UXers on my team. Hardly a day goes by where I don't connect a conversation topic to a recent episode I've enjoyed on my commute or when walking the dog. While I usually listen to general-interest podcasts and podcasts focused on making better decisions, the following are some podcasts and episodes specific to UX:

- *UI Breakfast* with Jane Portman is a broader design podcast, but she has at least two episodes dedicated to UXW, one with yours truly (https://bkaprt.com/buxw43/06-15). She is an excellent host who asks exactly what you'd ask if you could sit down with the people on the podcast. When you're looking for a new design rabbit hole, peruse the titles in her archive.
- *The Content Strategy Podcast* (https://bkaprt.com/buxw43/06-16) with Kristina Halvorson, CEO of Brain Traffic and producer of the Confab and Button conferences, is always in touch with current events and sentiments in content worldwide. They keep their ear to the ground so you can be in the know.
- The *NN/g UX Podcast* (https://bkaprt.com/buxw43/06-17) is a well-established source for broader UX topics.
- *Writers of Silicon Valley* (https://bkaprt.com/buxw43/06-18) with Patrick Stafford is no longer producing new episodes, but the archive covers a very relevant collection of topics with insightful guests in the UXW space. In particular, check out this excellent episode on accessibility with Shayla Byrd (https://bkaprt.com/buxw43/06-19).

String-management tools

I've attended many meetups where writers asked if anyone had a good system for managing strings (that wasn't Google Docs), and I always came up empty. Voice and tone management has always been a challenge, but thankfully a number of startups have arrived on the scene to address our pain. Here are some string-management tools I've found helpful:

- Ditto (https://bkaprt.com/buxw43/06-20)
- FlyCode (https://bkaprt.com/buxw43/06-21)
- Frontitude (https://bkaprt.com/buxw43/06-22)
- Strings (https://bkaprt.com/buxw43/06-23)

Other writing tools

- Content Design London's Readability Guidelines (https://bkaprt.com/buxw43/06-24) are an evidence-based, crowd-sourced collection of best practices for making our content readable.
- Writer (https://bkaprt.com/buxw43/05-02) is more about voice and tone style guide management—a tool for ensuring guideline application and consistency—than it is about integrating with design and code.
- Balsamiq (https://bkaprt.com/buxw43/06-25) is a wireframing tool I've used to work through content structure in the lowest fidelity phase of planning a user experience.
- The A11Y Project (https://bkaprt.com/buxw43/06-26) has a rich, community-driven collection of resources to make creating accessible digital experiences easier.
- The Mailchimp Content Style Guide (https://bkaprt.com/buxw43/05-04) has been the gold standard in UX writing for a long time, particularly when talking about voice and tone best practices. For that reason, and because their style guide is easy to use and publicly available, I used it as a model for the one I created at Fundbox.

More from me

I share content beyond the scope of this book in various places online. If you've enjoyed reading this, you might also want to check out the following:

- My Twitter feed (https://bkaprt.com/buxw43/06-27)
- My blog posts (https://bkaprt.com/buxw43/06-28)
- My website (https://bkaprt.com/buxw43/06-29)

REFERENCES

Shortened URLs are numbered sequentially; the related long URLs are listed below for reference.

Introduction

00-01 https://www.ted.com/talks/doug_dietz_the_design_thinking_journey_using_empathy_to_turn_tragedy_into_triumph

Chapter 1

01-01 https://www.nngroup.com/articles/100-years-ux

01-02 https://www.youtube.com/watch?v=DIGfwUt53nI

01-03 https://podcasts.apple.com/us/podcast/strategic-ux-writing-w-content-strategist-torrey-podmajersky/id1351536285?i=1000500095278

01-04 https://docs.microsoft.com/en-us/typography/develop/word-recognition

01-05 https://www.youtube.com/watch?v=DIGfwUt53nI

01-06 https://www.strings.design/blog/the-past-present-and-future-of-ux-writing-and-content-design-an-interview-with-kristina-halvorson

Chapter 2

02-01 https://www.fullstory.com/

02-02 https://www.usertesting.com/

02-03 https://costofdelay.com/cost-of-delay

02-04 https://anchor.fm/nngroup/episodes/5--ROI-The-Business-Value-of-UX-feat--Kate-Moran--Sr--UX-Specialist-at-NNg-en5ff7

02-05 https://www.nngroup.com/articles/three-myths-roi-ux

Chapter 3

03-01 https://www.nngroup.com/articles/calculating-roi-design-projects/

03-02 https://articles.uie.com/three_hund_million_button/

03-03 https://www.confabevents.com/2021-segments/stop-worrying-about-when-youre-included-and-start-doing-the-work

03-04 https://www.youtube.com/watch?v=FUXZZSa8Igk

03-05 http://bokardo.com/archives/writing-microcopy

03-06 https://www.nngroup.com/articles/do-interface-standards-stifle-design-creativity/

03-07 https://www.st-andrews.ac.uk/hr/edi/disability/facts/

03-08 https://www.w3.org/TR/WCAG21/

03-09 https://www.invisionapp.com/inside-design/writing-accessi-ble-microcopy/

03-10 https://hemingwayapp.com/

03-11 https://readabilityguidelines.myxwiki.org/xwiki/bin/view/Main/

03-12 https://accessibe.com/

Chapter 4

04-01 https://www.nngroup.com/articles/calculating-roi-design-projects/

04-02 http://confirmshaming.tumblr.com/

04-03 https://www.bbc.co.uk/gel/guidelines/how-research-is-different-for-ux-writing

04-04 https://vwo.com/success-stories/zalora

04-05 https://uxplanet.org/the-abcs-of-measuring-the-user-experience-of-your-product-or-service-f079d0676d5e

04-06 https://www.bbc.co.uk/gel/guidelines/how-research-is-different-for-ux-writing

04-07 http://webusability.com/firstclick-usability-testing

04-08 https://www.usability.gov/how-to-and-tools/methods/first-click-testing.html

04-09 http://neoinsight.com/about-us/case-studies/16-static-content/corporate/about-us/45-first-click-libraries

Chapter 5

05-01 https://courses.utterlycontent.com/p/content-operations-masterclass

05-02 https://writer.com/

05-03 https://www.grammarly.com/

05-04 https://styleguide.mailchimp.com

05-05 https://www.chatbot.com/chatbot-guide

05-06 https://www.hillary.black

05-07 https://www.interaction-design.org/literature/topics/voice-us-er-interfaces

Resources

06-01   https://abookapart.com/products/accessibility-for-everyone

06-02   https://contentdesign.london/store/the-content-design-book

06-03   https://abookapart.com/products/conversational-design

06-04   https://abookapart.com/products/cultivating-content-design

06-05   https://www.oreilly.com/library/view/dont-make-me/9780133597271

06-06   https://abookapart.com/products/just-enough-research

06-07   https://redish.net/books/letting-go-of-the-words

06-08   https://www.microcopybook.com/

06-09   https://abookapart.com/products/presenting-design-work

06-10   https://torreypodmajersky.com/strategic-writing-for-ux/

06-11   https://www.writingisdesigning.com/

06-12   https://www.buttonconf.com

06-13   https://www.confabevents.com/

06-14   https://www.utterlycontent.com/

06-15   https://uibreakfast.com/155-writing-microcopy-with-yael-ben-david

06-16   https://www.contentstrategy.com/

06-17   https://anchor.fm/nngroup

06-18   https://www.writersofsiliconvalley.com/

06-19   https://www.writersofsiliconvalley.com/episodes/2020/3/3/accessibili-ty-and-diversity-ux-writing-shayla-byrd

06-20   https://www.dittowords.com/

06-21   http://flycode.com/

06-22   https://www.frontitude.com/

06-23   https://www.strings.design/

06-24   https://readabilityguidelines.co.uk/

06-25   https://balsamiq.com/

06-26   https://www.a11yproject.com/

06-27   https://twitter.com/YaelBenDavid

06-28   https://yaelbendavid.medium.com/

06-29   https://www.yaelbendavid.me/

INDEX

A

A/B testing 78
accessibility 64-65
Arnold, Joshua 40

B

Bailey, Bob 82
benchmarks 71
best practices 9-15
bias 74-76
Black, Hillary 109
brand perception 64

C

call to action (CTA) 11
card sorting 84-86
click tests 81-83
cloze tests 92
collaboration 20-24
collaboration cycle 50-54
content documentation 97
content management system (CMS)
    100
content ops 97-101
content processes 98-99
content style guide (CSG) 100
contributing ideas 48-50
conversation design 107-110
customer acquisition cost (CAC) 89

D

Dietz, Doug 1
diversity, equity, and inclusion (DEI)
    67

F

fallback 64
friction 55-59

G

goals
    approval 28
    development 27-28
    documentation 26-27
graphical user interfaces (GUIs) 109

H

Hall, Erika 34, 108
Halvorson, Kristina 18
highlighter tests 92

I

inclusivity 67-68

K

KAPOW (framework) 30, 110
knowledge-sharing 15-16

L

lifetime value (LTV) 64, 73-74
localization 68-69

M

metrics 71
Metts, Michael J. 18
microcopy 4
Moran, Kate 43, 46, 72
motivation 59-62

N

net promoter score (NPS) 80
Norman, Don 6

O

open text surveys 89

P

PC revolution 5
Pearl, Cathy 110
Podmajersky, Torrey 9, 24, 71
Porter, Joshua 57
process 110-115
product requirements document
       (PRD) 115

Q

qualitative metrics 87-95
quality control 107
quantitative metrics 78-86

R

reputation 63-68
return on investment (ROI) 8, 46
RICE (framework) 32-34

S

scannability 10
single ease question (SEQ) 80
So, Preston 110
Spencer, Donna 77
Spool, Jared 46

T

technical barriers 57-59

U

usability testing 89-91
user experience (UX) 6
user experience writing (UXW) 1
user interviews 88
UX writing framework 30

V

van der Merwe, Greta 49
voice and tone 101-107
voice user interfaces (VUIs) 109

W

Walsh, Sarah 55
Web Content Accessibility Guidelines
       (WCAG) 65
web revolution 6
Welfle, Andy 18
Winters, Sarah 16, 24

Y

Yifrah, Kinneret 9, 102

ABOUT A BOOK APART

We cover the emerging and essential topics in web design and development with style, clarity, and above all, brevity—because working designer-developers can't afford to waste time.

COLOPHON

The text is set in FF Yoga and its companion, FF Yoga Sans, both by Xavier Dupré. Headlines and cover are set in Titling Gothic by David Berlow.

 This book was printed in the United States using FSC certified papers.

Yael Ben-David is a UX writer and content design leader who specializes in complex products. She is passionate about making innovative tech accessible to mass markets through clear, effective, data-driven copy. Yael loves the unique challenge of creating intentional and intricate experiences, and speaks about her work at meetups and conferences, and in masterclasses and university courses. After bouncing around the world a bit, Yael landed in Israel with a BA in journalism and an MSc/PhD in neurobiology, a husband, three kids, and a dog.

CPSIA information can be obtained
at www.ICGtesting.com
Printed in the USA
LVHW070402190723
752483LV00015B/467